For Sue
Thanks for your companionship and support around all
those racecourses
Not forgetting the apostrophes

Four Hooves and a Prayer

Racehorse ownership on a shoestring

Stephen A. Cawley

ISBN: 1523695226
ISBN 13: 9781523695225

Contents

Acknowledgements

THANKS TO STAN Hey's book for the original idea and the following sources have been used for reference purposes.

An Arm and Four Legs, Stan Hey, Yellow Jersey Press, 1998

Rock Of Gibraltar, Martin Hannan, Cutting Edge, 2004

The Course Inspector, Alan Lee, CollinsWillow, 2001

and the following web addresses

eliteracingclub.co.uk

ownaracehorse.co.uk

racegoersclub.co.uk

racingpost.com

skysports.com

sportinglife.com

Introductory Notes

AFTER AN INTRODUCTORY chapter explaining how the horse ownership on a shoestring project came about, there are five main chapters that follow the progress of each of the horses.

Each of these chapters follows the same template : an introduction to the horse, an outline of the race day at a particular racecourse, a description of the race and a postscript on what subsequently happened to the horse.

For those with limited knowledge of the sport I have included a glossary at the back of the book. In basic terms the horses followed in this book are flat and jumps racehorses. Flat racing means no jumps or hurdles, just a flat out gallop from start to finish. Jumps are racing over obstacles, either fences known as chases or hurdles. Of course the aim of the race is to win it, but it tends not to be such a straight-forward exercise!.

1
All Roads Start Here

HORSE RACING WAS never in my blood. I cannot wax lyrical and tell tales about trips to famous stables or racecourses in my formative years. Lester Piggot and the Grand National was about the sum total of my awareness of the world of racing. Indeed, as a sports- mad youngster there was possibly even some antipathy towards the sport of kings. I shamefully recollect now the quiet satisfaction I derived from the absence of the gee- gees, usually a staple on the famous *Grandstand* sports programme, due to the terrible outbreak of foot-and-mouth disease in 1967.

Summer holidays back in the land of my parents' birthplace, the Emerald Isle, did not introduce me to any equine talent. The land out west didn't seem to support much other than cattle and sheep, and they were barely noticed by an urbanite Mancunian. Indeed, many years later, when my favourite cousin leased out two of his fields, which we were told rather dubiously were for racehorses, they were deemed too far away for me to bother inspecting.

Growing up in Manchester, horse racing was virtually nonexistent. My mother would always make attempts at jollification. After we got a television in 1963, we would run a simple sweepstakes on the Grand National each year. Indeed it is possible that an early influence might have been gazing at a grainy black-and-white picture of the famous running of the 1967 National, which resulted in Foinavon winning at odds of 100–1. Looking back on it, there was something pretty dramatic about the race as described in the dulcet tones of the erudite Peter O'Sullivan and the manic Michael O'Hehir, who told of the carnage of that twenty-third fence that seemed to lead to all the field falling and the no-hoper being left to gallop away and win the race.

There must have been some subliminal influence at work in the house because our cat was called Arkle. This meant little to me at the time, but reading about Arkle the horse subsequently, he was clearly something of a celebrity of the day, and I feel the cat's moniker probably had a lot to do with national pride. Michael D. Higgins is quoted as saying, "Everyone remembers Arkle." And Ian Balding reinforces the widely held view that he was "the greatest racehorse of all time." In those less clustered days of television sport, "Himself" was up there with the likes of Mohammad Ali as sport stars who defied the dictate that sport was always consigned to the back pages.

For the adult males I knew in my adolescent years in Manchester, horse racing existed merely as a list of names in the inside back pages of the *Manchester Evening News*. The sport seemed to be purely a betting medium. I don't think these men ever saw the horses run; they were simply a topic of conversation on the way to and from the public house. In all likelihood, they checked the results in the bookies and lamented the fact that they had seen the winner in the evening news but had chosen another horse!.

Football was my number-one sporting passion. When, once fortnightly, one could take in the holy trinity of Charlton, Law, and Best, who needed horses?

It was not until I was in gainful employment with the Sheffield education committee that I suddenly began to glimpse the exotic potential of horse racing. My new teaching colleague (and lifelong racing acquaintance), Les, seemed to have had a very different upbringing than I did; he was steeped in the sport with what seemed to me to be an encyclopedic knowledge of the horses. I joined Les on what seemed like a national tour of England's racecourses, but my transformation into a racing fan was gradual. My new mate seemed to know every aspect there was to know about horses, except the knack of winning! He seemed to take ages poring over the *Sporting Life*, assessing all the horse form before making the most careful of selections, yet virtually every horse he picked found all sorts of novel ways to lose the race!

My burgeoning interest in the sport was stimulated to some extent by this wagering aspect. In a way that mystified Les, I seemed to be able to pick 'em without recourse to any such study. One of my first spectacular coups was a horse called Oh I Oyston (owned and named by the family, linked to their less-than-successful owner-ship of the Blackpool football club). When this horse romped home at 33–1, Les sat back stupefied, not least because of the fact that I had opted for the horse because I liked the name! In case there was any doubt that this was beginner's luck, I quickly repeated the trick with Von Trapps Express, and over the years, I would randomly come up with similar long-odds winners.

My burgeoning interest in racing was stimulated to some extent by this wagering aspect. But there was no need for my mother to worry that such initial luck was going to lead to a life of gambling addiction, as my stake both then and now was always a small one. On this first occasion, the winnings just stretched toward buying an extra round of drinks—beer, not champagne. My innate caution mixed with my desire to remain solvent meant there was never any danger that I could have been the next Harry Findlay or J. P. McManus (men famed for their gambling exploits).

I nonetheless retained an ability to pick the odd long shot in the odds, often for the sketchiest of reasons, usually related to names, numbers, or colours. My son's name is Joe, and it's uncanny how many horses named Joe have won for me—certainly a figure in excess of 75 percent. Unfortunately, one thing I quickly noted was that each spectacular success was usually followed by a long line of losers.

It was only in later years, when my education was complete, so to speak, that I realised that lucky punting had to be supplemented by more serious study. Now I knew what to look for: age, going, weight, previous form, the racecourse, trainer, jockey, and so on. I would spend similarly long periods of time deciding on my selections. I realised there was a lot to take into account, whether it was a group race or a handicap, and indeed this knowledge and awareness became part of the enjoyment of a day at the races.

Nonetheless, even after all the study is done, I will still assess whether or not any of those "lucky" factors are at play, and if one is, it becomes the deciding factor. Over the past ten years, a day at the races has become a much more regular outing, especially if it is a jumps meeting. One could say I had become smitten. I was immediately struck by the colourful nature of the event and the sense of occasion.

Before you get to the course, the all-important "form" study enables you to construct the short list. Then there is the spectacle of the parade ring in advance of the race, when you can see the listed horses at close quarters, followed by the dramatic denouement of the race itself, hopefully with "your horse" leading them all home. (Well, it happens sometimes). Finally, all of the horses return to the winner's enclosure, where speeches and presentations round the occasion off in the proper order.

Watching such a spectacle, either on the television or at the racecourse, was the sum total of my involvement with the sport of kings, but wandering into a secondhand bookstore five or so years ago changed all that. My eyes alighted on a little paperback with a catchy title. It was called *An Arm and Four Legs*, and the subtitle was *A Journey into Racehorse Ownership*. This was an amusing account of the attempts of a journalist (Stan Hey) and his well-connected media mates to buy into a couple of National Hunt racehorses in the early 1990s. Hey bought quite a substantial share in the horses, if memory serves me right, somewhere around 25 percent, at quite a cost. Horse ownership was not an inexpensive hobby, and he seemed to have spent some thousands of pounds on two horses because he had long cherished the idea of having his "own" horse and seeing it at the races. Basically, the book outlined the amusing and at times farcical frustrations the author had to withstand in what amounted to the trials and tribulations of horse ownership. Either the horse never or rarely got as far as the race track after a long and costly preparation, or the horse perhaps shouldn't have made it to the racecourse due to their lamentable attempts to win a race.

Despite this gloomy scenario, the book left a deep impression on me and got me thinking about the nature of horse ownership. It seemed to me that these grammar-school lads' move into the previously exclusive world of horse ownership was a noble and worthwhile venture. The author was clearly imbued with, shall we say, a mediacelebrity-style lifestyle. He was capable of throwing large sums of money at his passion for horses, either in the purchase and training of them or the alcoholic excesses that usually characterised his visits to the racecourse. What was it that so cheered him, despite the fact that he had a horrendous run of fortune with the horses he "owned" and despite the massive cost deficit he seemed to have at the end of the experience? Well, he clearly enjoyed his day out at the races, with his "owner's badge" glistening in the sun. He was definitely much more involved than he had been when he was merely a punter at the races. He constantly maintained an optimism that the day would come when he would be accompanying his horse into the winner's enclosure.

Despite a farcical run of nonevents, Hey maintained his optimism, succinctly summing up his ownership experience this way: "Owners develop an innate sense of the value that they are getting from their involvement with horses, one that doesn't involve prize money or winning from bets. The value comes in all sorts of ways—the escape from drudgery or pressure, the good-humoured camaraderie of the racecourse, and the necessary triumph of optimism over cynicism. Try putting a price on these."

His experiences put the germ of an idea in my mind. Surely if the premise of ownership was to acquire a share in a horse (no matter how small) which thus enabled one to be informed about how the horse was training and then eventually go to see "your" horse run at a racecourse, then this could be done without throwing large amounts of money at it. Indeed, one could take the opposite tack to Stan Hey's approach and choose the syndicated, large membership groups that so put him off. A little bit of homework on my part showed there were lots of these "cheap" ownership options available and that with any luck, I might well see much better horses than Mr. Hey encountered—and who knows, maybe get to a more exotic range of racecourses. Pragmatism dictated that for the kind of money I was likely to spend (hundreds rather than Mr. Hey's thousands), I would have to tweak my template slightly. I decided I would select five horses over different time periods in a two-year time frame. I would endeavour to monitor the horses' progress from training and prep races to the racecourse. For each horse, I would target a particular race and obtain an owner's badge for that race, and who knows, maybe even end up in the winner's enclosure.

I would be owner for a day, and in so doing, I would be able to assess what these racecourses offered to people at my new exalted status. Of course Mr. Hey had rejected this route as almost "too cheap," but if it achieved the very things he had sought at a fraction of the cost, it was worth a go. My story about horse ownership on a shoestring had begun.

2
All Roads Lead To Haydock Park

DOYLY CARTE WAS a mare running in the distinctive black-and-white silks of the Elite Racing Club. Founded in 1992, the club now proudly proclaimed themselves to be Britain's ; "'all- time most successful racing club'."

    The concept behind the club was simple: mass ownership of a lot of horses at a very affordable price. The aim was to have a string, composed of both jumps and flat horses, stabled with some of the country's leading trainers. This, of course, was the direct opposite of Mr. Hey's individual ownership model, as there were thousands of members of the Elite Racing Club. The club would keep members informed about the "string" via a weekly newsletter and a website. In theory, therefore, one could see the horses in various stable visits and experience the thrill of being "owner for a day" by seeing one of the horses race. Stan Hey had mentioned the club when he was examining his options at the start of his book, but he said he had decided that given the membership numbers, he was unlikely to actually see one of the horses run. I, however, came to the absolutely opposite conclusion. If "ownership on a shoestring" was my goal, the club met my requirements exactly, and I felt that with appropriate tactics, I would see exactly the horse I wanted to on the racecourse. I was impressed by the size of the club's string, the geographical spread of the trainers, and although it may have been a diluted version of Mr. Hey's ownership model, the quality of the horses was likely to be higher than any he encountered.

The real success of the club was in its breeding operation. Over the years of its existence, it had built up its own stock of broodmares and had consequently bred its own racehorses; and some had been very good. This appealed to the football fan in me, as my own football team's rich history had been characterised by developing its own talent.,.the "Busby babes" and Fergusons's "class of '92" had showed what was possible with a little patience. Given the size, scale, and wealth of Elite's "opposition" in the horse-breeding and ownership world, I decided it was an organisation worth supporting. The club's most famous home-bred was a horse called Soviet Song, a five-time Group One winner in the noughties and a clear affirmation of the club's success.

Stan Hey had felt that the club was too "Southern-based and flat-horse oriented," and, given his ownership plans, "just too cheap!" However, given the premise of my own research and the value-for-money maxim, I felt that it met all my requirements. I decided I would choose three of the clubs horses from the outset and follow them over two years. Taking each horse over a part of that set time period, I would follow the horses progress in terms of training and career and, of course, be "owner for the day" by going to see the horse run. Despite Mr. Hey's concerns about a flat bias, the club appeared to have a good hurdler on their books, trained in the North and already doing well. Her name was Doyly Carte, and she possessed the potential to do even better.

Doyly was one of the club's homebred horses, being out of Generous Diana and sired by Doyen. She was trained by the North's leading trainer of the day, Donald McCain. The McCain name was synonymous with Britain's most famous horse race, the Grand National. Donald's father, Donald "Ginger" McCain, had won the National three times with Red Rum, which he had famously trained from a tiny yard behind a car showroom in Southport. In later years, when more established, he won it again with Amberleigh House. His son, Donald McCain junior, carried on the family tradition, by winning the National in 2011 with Ballabriggs. Although the father might have put the McCain name on the horse-racing map, it was Junior who had established himself by 2012 as the North's leading trainer. His operation was on an altogether larger scale, with a quality string of more than a hundred horses, including horses that had won at jumping's blue riband meeting, Cheltenham, in March. At the time, McCain was in the middle of four seasons when he had recorded more than one hundred winners. In value terms, he was the country's third-ranked National Hunt trainer. Stable visits to see Doyly revealed just how far the training operation had moved on since the Southport days. Now based at the luxurious Bankhouse stables in the shadow of Cholmondeley Castle, the yard was the epitome of a modern training facility. Doyly, a big mare but seemingly with an equitable temperament, seemed at home in her high-tech environment.

Donald appeared to think a lot of her. As she went through her paces on the woodchip gallops, he had gone as far as tipping her as one of his many horses to follow in one of the various racing mags that stimulate the optimism in advance of many a National Hunt season.

Doyly had impressed from the start, winning her first race, a bumper (a flat race, run under NH rules), at Catterick in January 2012. Her form was so impressive in her first couple of races that she made it to a listed (if won, this would distinguish the quality animal from the pit pony) mares bumper at Aintree's showcase April meeting. Although she was halfway down that twenty-runner field, there was clearly a good deal of potential in this talented half sister to the club's star flat horse of the time, Dandino. I began to take an active interest in her progress from November 2012, when there appeared to be much excitement that she might become a very decent hurdler. Doyly didn't disappoint, winning both of her first two starts over hurdles. A mare's maiden hurdle at Mussleborough was won very easily by eleven lengths, and Doyly followed this with another maiden mare's hurdle, but this time at a higher Class Four race at Catterick. By the turn of the year, only the heavy going at Taunton had slowed down her progress, but the British Horse racing Authority recognised her talent. Having now run three times over hurdles, she was allocated a respectable mark of 118.(In National Hunt Classification, this would have enabled her to run in class 3 races. Class 1 is the highest standard, class 6 is the lowest).

Doyly maintained her upward momentum in her next race. Her third-place finish at Sedgefield was a little frustrating; she had looked set to win, but the tank emptied on the run in, and she was third to Runswick Royal. However, it was Doyly's eighth career run that really made people sit up. At National Hunt headquarters Cheltenham, she won a prestigious "listed" race, a mares' hurdle at the juicy odds of 13–2. Traveling in her usual easy style and jumping fluently, she stayed on well up that famous finishing stretch to beat the hot favorite, the well-regarded Ma Filleule.

This was, as they say, a "taking" performance. I was more than impressed as I stood in the bookies', grasping my winnings. Elite had a pretty good hurdler on their hands. The handicapper duly took note, and Doyly finished the 2012–2013 season with a mark of 131. Donald McCain professed himself "really pleased." A summer's rest would allow the horse to strengthen and improve further. Although tempted to now "put in" for an owner's badge, I decided to wait further into the next season, when Doyly could be in a really big race. But there was nothing to stop me from going along to watch her progress before that moment arrived.

Indeed, at the start of November of the new season, I took in Doyly's first run at Wetherby. It proved to be an underwhelming performance. Was this a reality check or merely an early-season glitch? Doyly could never get on terms and finished down the nine-runner field.

Despite not making the "frame" for the first time in her hurdling career, the fifth-place finish in a good-quality race (listed) meant that Doyly's mark went up again and now stood at 137. There was much talk of the horse having some serious targets to aim at; she was clearly a very good mare with a string of good results behind her. I decided now was the time to put in for that owner's badge, and I was encouraged to see that a possible race had been earmarked at nearby Haydock Park. However, at this stage, this was merely an aspiration on the part of the trainer. The prospect was an enticing one. The November meeting was one of the highlights of the early jumping calendar and would feature a potentially top-class Lancashire chase.

Of course I was aware of Mr. Hey's comment that the eleven thousand-plus members of the club would make my precise aspiration something of a speculative gamble, but isn't that what horse racing is all about? I had, after all, employed some tactical nous in my planning, having purposely held back from applying to see any club horses run, on the basis that when I did "strike," I would maximise my chances. I had also deduced from comments in the newsletter that at some race meetings, the owner's badge allocation had not always been fully taken up. It could be that some of the 'thousands' enjoyed various aspects of the club but didn't always go to the races.

When Doyly was declared on Friday, November 22nd, to run at Haydock, I took my chance and applied for the owner's badge. I had actually been racing at Haydock on that Friday for the only time in my life, winning the placepot bet and the princely sum of thirty pounds. I considered this a lucky omen, and I placed my request for a badge through the club's website and awaited the outcome. When Saturday, November 23rd dawned, I went downstairs at the appointed time to check the Elite site and was delighted to see that my application had indeed been successful. Armed with the binoculars and with the *Racing Post* purchased, I set off on the first of "my 'ownership.' days."

What a prospect, seeing Doyly in a Class Two intermediate hurdle race! It was followed later in the afternoon by a top-class Betfair chase, which looked like a mini-Gold Cup, featuring such luminaries as Bobs Worth, Long Run, Silviniaco Conti, and Cue Card.

• • •

RACE DAY—DOYLY CARTE AT HAYDOCK, SATURDAY, NOVEMBER 23, 2013
THE RACECOURSE
Haydock Park, located in Merseyside, is one of the North's premier racetracks. Although located close to the urban metropolis of Liverpool and Manchester, the course itself is situated in parkland. The technical detail describes it as a flattened left-hand oval of one mile, five furlongs. It is regarded as a galloping course. This day's meeting was one of the early-season highlights of the jumping calendar, and we were part of a large crowd making our way to the course on that bright Saturday morning. Indeed, it was so large that we were clogged up in a traffic jam that caused a serious delay to my big day and necessitated some suicidal driving around the giant roundabout

that led to the course. Such kamikaze methods were needed to make the first race.

Eschewing the Tattersall entrance I had used the day before, we made our way to the more salubriously appointed county-stand entrance. Everything seemed very well organised, and on inquiry, I was presented with my badge and complimentary race programme. The attendants were used to large crowds and cheerfully gave instructions on where to find the paddock pavilion and where the owners' and trainers' bar was located. Any nervousness I might have had about entering this new environment was rapidly suppressed as I quickly located the bar. Drinking my complimentary tea, I quickly read the glossy programme. I knew that Mr. Hey was hardly likely to approve of my tea drinking, given the alcoholic excess of his race trips, but with real ale almost impossible to find on a British race-course, I felt I could afford the sacrifice.

On the opening page, General Manager Garry Fortune confirmed that this was some day to be making my ownership debut. "With the Betfair chase as the leading act, it promises to be a fantastic day," he declared. Gary said he wanted to wish all of "today's connections the best of luck." He probably had Mr. McManus or Mr. Hemmings in mind, but I took his best wishes personally. After all, there I was, a Lancashire lad enjoying the best of what the sport had to offer. Pretentious, *moi*?

The bar was quite cramped and extremely busy with various train-ers and owners moving briskly about and exchanging pleasantries. I stood agog, gripping my second cup of tea, when someone who looked very much like Nicky Henderson grabbed the biscuits I had my eye on. On striking up a conversation with the nearest chap, I was surprised to find that he was a fellow Elite member from Bolton. "Oh, yes," the fellow said, "been racing many times with Elite, and never been out of the frame." *Well,* I thought, *let's hope Doyly keeps his record intact.*

The owners, and particularly the trainers, seemed to watch the races from the Tommy Whittle stand that was part of the county enclosure. There were certainly clear views of the course and the winning line from this vantage point. I was a little surprised, however, by the fact that the trainers seemed to be corralled into a small section of the stand. Sitting there, I couldn't help looking around and putting names to faces I'd previously spotted in the papers. Just below me was the distinctive figure of Venetia Williams, with her trademark black glasses on. As the first race finished, she skipped down the steps, looking particularly happy. That was not surprising, really, because her horse, Moujik Borget, had just won.

• • •

PRERACE
The parade ring at Haydock Park is quite spectacular. It is a large, tree-lined area with a good deal of space for the "connections" to meet up. Feeling a little self-conscious as I crossed the boundary line from my usual parade-ring viewing spot, I entered the inner sanctum for the first time. With my newly acquired friend from Elite at my side, we quickly located the other Elite "owners," who were distinguished by the fact the size of their group dwarfed all other ownership groups. They seemed to be knowledgeable racegoing folk, and some seemed very familiar with the protocol of this ownership lark. Elite make a bit of a fuss about dress code, and looking around me, the members seemed to have adhered to their wishes, with all in eminently sensible clothing.

Donald McCain seemed to be in the know, and he made his way toward us as the horses paraded around the outside of the ring.

Doyly was beautifully turned out. To my uneducated eyes, she looked like the picture of equine health. Other members murmured about her obvious well-being, saying she was "on her toes" and had "never looked better." Donald McCain's manner was avuncular, at least on the surface. Ever ready with a quip, he seemed to have perfected a jokey countenance that put all at ease. His comments regarding Doyly were more circumspect. He told us she was in good condition, but bearing in mind the quality of the race, he said, "Let's just see what happens." Jason McGuire, McCain's regular jockey, now appeared at his side. Focused but polite, he introduced himself to the enthusiastic group of owners. Following these pleasantries, Donald and Jason moved away from us and toward Doyly, and some last-minute instructions appeared to be administered.

It was a small field of five, but as a Class Two race, its quality was unmistakable, with many dangers, it appeared, to Doyly. Elite's sister company, Axom, offers syndicate ownership to much smaller exclusive groups, but with a much heftier price tag. Axom had a horse named Far West that was, trained by champion trainer Paul Nichols.

Second in the previous season's triumph hurdle, he was a hot favourite at close to even money. As if this was not enough, the other giant of the National Hunt training world, Nicky Henderson, was running Rolling Star, who had been the favourite in that Triumph race, finishing sixth.

If Morning Royalty offered less imposing opposition to our mare, with a BHA mark seven pounds below Doyly, Runswick Royal reminded all what a tough race this was; she had already beaten Doyly at Sedgefield. Most of the racing pundits had tipped Far West. Doyly didn't seem to enter calculations and was freely available at 16-1. I wasn't going to let these doomsayers ruin such a glorious day.

Looking through their selections at races, I was always struck by how few tips they actually got right. Maybe today was another day when they would call it wrong. Undeterred I placed a crisp twenty-pound note on the nose as they say, misplaced loyalty possibly, but I felt the occasion demanded it.

• • •

THE RACE—BETFAIR HURDLE (CLASS TWO), 2 MILES
Watching Doyly Carte from the owner's section of the stand at Haydock was an exhilarating experience, not least because the mare ran the race of her life.

Making nonsense of the prerace odds, the mare ran a grand race, coming to the last with every chance of winning. Early in the race, I was pleased that our horse seemed so positive and seemed to be taking to her fences with real confidence. She quickly moved in to a prominent position, close to the head of affairs under a determined and positive ride by Jason, and she seemed to be running the finish out of the favourite, Far West, who was toiling in her rear. As they passed me at the end of the first circuit, the enjoyment of just being there was surpassed by an increasing awareness that we had a real chance in the race. By the second last fence, her fluent jumping had taken her to the front. I began to think the impossible was on, as the others were clearly in trouble. Scarcely able to believe what I was seeing, the commentator confirmed that Doyly was making all, and I began to shout myself hoarse as the horse maintained her momentum, jumping the second last cleanly and heading for home. Unfortunately, it was at just this point that I saw Barry Geraghty galvanise his mount, Rolling Star. In what seemed an instant, he had quickly closed the gap and drawn up level with Doyly as they jumped the last. Coming away from that fence, Rolling Star took the lead, and although Doyly bravely stayed on, she couldn't get her lead back. Rolling Star won by a couple of lengths.

The final placings saw Rolling Star win at odds of 5-2, with Doyly Carte second and Runswick Royal finishing third. The hot favourite Far West could only manage fourth place, a neck ahead of Morning Royalty who finished fifth.

• • •

POSTRACE

Any immediate disappointment soon dissipated as the syndicate quickly gathered back in the parade ring. There was much cheering and applause as Doyly was proudly brought to the post allocated for second place. Jason was quick to praise the horse; he declared that she had given him a "great ride."

A pleased-looking Donald McCain said, "I told Jason to keep it simple, and he did just that." The "owners" were certainly an elated bunch now. Many patted the horse and told her how well she had done. "She's a certainty for the mares' hurdle at Cheltenham now," opined one lady.

"Yes, if she can live with those horses she could do well," claimed another.

The man I had met earlier in the day was quick to remind me of his boast that he was never out of the winner's enclosure on his "owner-ship" days. He was quick to add, "And we beat the Axom lot!"

It was a good race to come second in, and the £7,392, was more money than would usually accrue for first place in many a standard hurdle race. Once the deductions would be made for transport and for trainer and jockey fees, there would be winnings for all those thousands of members to share. Well, a couple of quid might come my way later in the year. Money didn't come into it, though; that was quite an experience as the first of the "ownership" days. All that was left was to return to the owners' room, grab some more biscuits and tea, and later on enjoy a top-class Betfair chase, won by Cue Card.

• • •

POSTSCRIPT—DOYLY CARTE

Following Doyly's wonderful run at Haydock, she achieved her highest-ever BHA rating of 140, a mark she lived up to when second to the Irish superstar mare of the time, Annie Power, at Doncaster, two months later. The lady who had claimed that Doyly was good enough for the Cheltenham festival saw her words borne out as Doyly made it to the mares' hurdle at Cheltenham. I was there to see her take her place in a sixteen-runner field, not with my "owner's" hat on, but as a proud Elite member. She had done well to get to the high point of the year for all jump-racing fans, but she was up against it, with the imperious Quevega at the head of the betting. Bad news had preceded her arrival when her regular jockey, Jason McGuire, sustained terrible injuries the day before and was to be out for some time. A mixture of loyalty and expectation enveloped me as I placed ten pounds each way on her. But unfortunately, her opponents all went a bit quick for her, and she trailed finishing in fourteenth place.

We didn't know it then, but Haydock was to mark Doyly's high water mark. Life from then on was to get much harder. By November 2014, a year after Haydock, Donald McCain's long-term plan to send Doyly chasing had come to fruition. On a stable visit, he seemed convinced that Doyly would turn into a "lovely chaser."

It was not to be, as Doyly never seemed to relish the bigger obstacles. A fall at Catterick in December seemed to dent her confidence. When she unceremoniously offloaded her jockey at Musselburgh two months later, the writing seemed to be on the wall. I had been a little surprised by the decision to go chasing when she had proved to be such a proficient hurdler, but it would seem that her size and scope meant such progression was inevitable.

In an attempt to ignite the spark, Doyly was returned to hurdling. However, a series of lacklustre showings that included two "pulled-up" efforts brought about the dreaded e-mail pronouncement from the trainer that Doyly had "fallen out of love" with racing. This is a euphemism that trainers seem to use when they feel the game is up and further progress, shall we say, is questionable.

I had seen the term before in relation to other horses, and it nearly always spelled the end of their racing career.

It was a deflating end to a career that had looked so promising just twelve months before. But her record reflected what a good horse she had been, with a 21 percent strike rate of four wins in nineteen races and winnings of more than £40,000. Elite had resisted the urge to breed from Doyly and decided to recoup some more money by sending her to the December 2015 mares' sale at the Tattersalls breeding-stock sales. She had a pleasant preparation period of some months at the Furnace Mill stud in Warwickshire. Given Doyly's role as the first horse of my "ownership" days, I felt the least I could do was to go and see how she was getting on. So in August 2015, I went over to the spectacularly located Furnace Mill.

Doyly was paraded in front of some members on that sunny Saturday, and from what I could see, she appeared content; she was certainly very well turned out. No doubt she was a "back number" now, in racing terms, but to me she was the talented horse I had picked randomly from Elite's string who had got this ownership saga underway and given us such a memorable day at Haydock Park, and for that I would always remember her

Doyly Carte was sold at the December breeding-stock sales for £30,000.

3
All Roads Lead To Longchamp

RIBBONS, IN MANY ways, was what the Elite Racing Club was all about and what they had specialised in since 1998, when they had their first homebred winner.

Homebred Ribbons had a bloodline that went back through the club's most successful horse, Soviet Song, and back to Kalinka, one of the club's most influential foundation mares. Sister Act, Ribbons's dam, was the sister of the much-feted Soviet Song. Ribbons would become one of the club's greatest horses and the club's first horse to win a Group One race since her famous auntie.

That, however, was not the case in September 2012, when I joined the Elite Racing Club. Ribbons was unraced at the time, and although "beautifully bred," as they say (sired by Manduro), the club's star performer of the day was Dandino. Ribbons's trainer was the well-regarded James Fanshawe, who had trained Soviet Song in her pomp and was also training Dandino to great effect. Dandino appeared to be a top-class horse with winnings around the £400,000 mark and seemed to be aimed at some good-quality races, both at home and abroad. Despite these achievements, it was Ribbons that grabbed my attention. Given her impeccable breeding line and potential, I decided to make her the second horse in this ownership exercise and follow her from scratch, so to speak.

As each newsletter and e-mail arrived from Elite, I focused intently on what was being said about Ribbons. At this point, Ribbons was a two-year-old but had not thus far run in this flat season. If she was to appear, I gathered it would be at the very tail end of the season. It was clear that James Fanshawe held the horse in some regard, but clearly not having appeared on the racecourse meant that her training progress had not been tested by the reality of a race. Therefore, many of Fanshawe's briefings had caution built into them: She was "quite weak" at present, "looked green" at times, and so on. As September moved into October, the option to run on turf seemed to diminish. Although Ribbons was getting it together, she remained quite weak. It was obviously the physical aspect of her development that was holding things back, but then as I had almost decided there would be no run for the horse, news came through that she would indeed make her debut. Clearly deciding that the turf options had all but disappeared, Ribbons was declared to run in a maiden fillies' race on the all-weather at Kempton.

There was some cautious optimism that Ribbons could run well, with the "value" given as 7–1, but I was left in no doubt that the main objective of the exercise was to get a "run" into the filly. As I went down to the bookies for the 5.55 pm race, it was noticeable how friendless Ribbons was. It was easy to get odds of 16–1, and I placed a modest amount on her, taking the prudent precaution of backing her each way. The weight of my investment clearly made little difference because shortly afterward, her odds moved out again, settling at 20–1. Despite the lack of support, she started well enough and seemed to be traveling very well but was held in the pack of horses who appeared to be set to envelop her. But then Ribbons shot through the pack of horses, accelerating away to win by the comfortable margin of two and a half lengths.

This was, as they say, a taking performance. One couldn't help be impressed with this performance, and I was delighted that my "chosen" horse had run so well.

James Fanshawe was not known for winning with first-time-out two-year-olds, and he declared himself "very pleased." We were going to have some fun with this one next season, it seemed.

So it proved. At the start of the 2013 flat season, Ribbons reeled off three wins on the trot, winning twice at Goodwood and once at Newmarket. I congratulated myself on choosing this horse. With Dandino now sold, Ribbons had suddenly emerged as the star of the string. Correspondingly, Ribbons's handicap mark had also begun to rise, but thus far, this had not stopped her winning. It had reached the respectable level of 86 (the figures used for flat horses are lower than national hunt, ranging from 0 to 110 plus, this figure would have enabled Ribbons to enter class 2 handicap races) when she ran at Goodwood, with the only blip that day being a few shenanigans, with the horse nearly refusing to start. Ribbons's winning run came to an end in September, when she finished third at Yarmouth.

Despite favouritism, she was never able to really put a challenge in. The consolation was this was a listed Class One race, and the third-place prize money was reasonable.

Ribbons was definitely a very good horse and clearly had her own distinctive style. She was a "holdup" horse. She liked the "cover" of the other horses and liked to pass them with a late burst toward the line. She preferred some give in the going, so some rain seemed a prerequisite. It seemed that a mile was to be her preferred distance. What was most noticeable was the manner in which she had been trained. Talking to some members at race events, I got the distinct impression that they wanted to see her race as often as possible, but James Fanshawe had a very patient approach. If conditions weren't right, the horse wouldn't be declared. I found this a fascinating insight into the trainer's mindset; he was clearly something of a perfectionist and wouldn't be rushed with such a good racehorse. He clearly felt that this method would enable Ribbons to maintain her top form longer.

I decided that with Ribbons being aimed at some high-class races in 2014, this would be the optimum time to attempt to get into the ownership ring. The season started with a run at Kempton in April and although she was performing in some top-class races, the opposition by definition was all the tougher. She was second in this race, coming through the field late again, but this time unable to catch the winner. She raced at Ascot in May in a fillies' handicap and indeed was favourite to win a good-quality contest. This time, however, the hold up tactics didn't quite work, and she failed reel in Amulet, losing by a neck. The handicapper continued to be impressed, however, and Ribbons's mark subsequently was raised to 99.

James Fanshawe had a habit of racing horses successfully in France, and Ribbons's next assignment was at Deauville in August. Ribbons was entered in the Prix Darley Jean Romanet stakes, a Group One race with a large prize-money pot. This was the first time the horse was ridden by the charismatic Frankie Dettori. They proved to be a dynamic partnership, with Ribbons available at 11-1, winning the race in style, with that characteristically deadly finish. This was a very significant win, both for the horse and the Elite Club. The horse had won more than €150,000 and now possessed the black type so crucial to her future. For the club it was their first Group One since the halcyon days of Soviet Song (who had in fact won five Group One races) and was clearly an affirmation of everything they had set out to do. From my point of view, I was amazed at just how well this horse had done from the moment I had followed her as a club yearling. Surely the time had come to enter the owner's ring and see the superstar for myself.

For a jumps fan who could take or leave the "flat" stuff, it takes some explanation to work out how I ended up in the owner's "ring" at Longchamp on Arc day. In terms of the premise behind this book, I cannot pretend that I simply "put in" to see Ribbons and subsequently turned up at Longchamp on the day widely regarded as the highlight of the flat-racing calendar. In truth, it needed a certain amount of forward planning and an awful lot of luck, a split of about 20/80 in percentage terms. It was clear to me that Ribbons's achievements had projected her into exalted company and that James Fanshawe liked to race his horses in France. I was also of the opinion that Ribbons liked cut in the ground and that Longchamp was renowned as a course that was well watered and rarely, if ever, firm going. On this, admittedly the sketchiest of plans, I booked to take in the 2014 Arc meeting five months before the event. I decided to take a package with the horse-racing-abroad company, through the good offices of Elite. My rationale at that point was that Ribbons was enjoying a promising season and did not appear to be targeted at a main race in the United Kingdom and that if the French idea was a pipedream, at least myself and my wife would get a nice holiday.

In characteristic fashion, James was very cautious with his entries and declarations. On a number of occasions, it seemed possible that Ribbons was going to run, only to be informed that conditions were not quite right. In fact, Ribbons was handled so carefully that she was due to go three months without appearing on a racecourse. Some members were frustrated by such caution, and the correspondence

pages of the newsletter were sometimes filled with carping comments. The situation was epitomised in September, when Ribbons
was entered but not declared at Haydock and was chosen to race at
Salisbury but in the end didn't race at all. While some members were
no doubt frustrated by this, I was pleased, as it seemed to me this
would increase her chances of running in France. The stunning win at
Deauville in August essentially did two things. It obviously brought
the plaudits of a Grade One success, but running so well in France
meant that there was serious talk now of going to Longchamp. Indeed,
for many weeks in advance, the club newsletter recorded that costly
advance entries had been made for Ribbons at Longchamp on Arc
day. By the time I set off for France, Ribbons remained entered and
likely to run, but with James Fanshawe, one couldn't be certain until
the "declaration" stage.

• • •

**RACE DAY—RIBBONS AT LONGCHAMP, SUNDAY, OCTOBER 5,
2014**
THE RACECOURSE
Longchamp, sited in the Bois de Boulogne on the outskirts of
Paris, is considered one of Europe's premier racecourses. On the
first weekend in October, it hosts the Prix de l'Arc de Triomphe,
arguably Europe's single most important flat race. The technical
details belie the majesty of the racecourse, a right-handed track
that runs around a one-mile, six-furlong circuit. It characteristically rises in the back straight and has a slight fall as it enters a
short home straight.

The horse- racing- abroad package had enabled us to use their
"exclusive"course pavilion, situated a couple of furlongs from the
finishing line. Although allowing access to all parts of the course,

the specific attraction it seemed was being in the 'Pavilion Des Anglais', which meant that, we were surrounded by all things English. Effectively, one was allocated a reserved seat, under cover, in an airy, well- constructed stand, with clear views of this wonderful course. Taking in the Saturday of the meeting enabled us to review the facilities available. Surprisingly, the French had not come in their thousands, so it was very easy to navigate and explore the parade ring and the resplendent stands. Our pavilion gave us a great view of the horses racing around the corner and fighting out the run in, if not the clearest view of the actual winning line. The pavilion, as it name suggests, was catering for the large influx of English racing fans who annually attend this meeting. With an English race commentary, Paris mutual betting facilities, television screens, a long bar, and various restaurants, one didn't actually need to leave the pavilion, some of the crowd clearly thought that was the best policy.

The Saturday had surprised me by being relatively quiet. It was very easy to walk around in the autumn sunshine and make my way from the pavilion to the very impressive parade ring. This was like a small amphitheatre, with steep banking, allowing hundreds of people to look down on the ring below. The thought struck me that I could be in that ring the next day, although at this stage we were still not certain that Ribbons would even run. The quality of the racing on Saturday was unmistakable. What was particularly noticeable was how many races seemed to be won in the final furlong; the thoroughbreds seemed to "switch on" as they approached the finishing line. My appetite whetted, late on Saturday night I applied through the club website for the owner's badge for the next day's racing, more in hope than expectation. My strategy of being in the right place at the right time had worked, but now I had to compete with all those thousands of members.

• • •

PRERACE

Regardless of how Ribbons might do in her race, I had "won" my individual prize when I checked the website to find my name listed. I was indeed to be one of Ribbons's owners on one of the most important days of her race career, and I would be in the ring on Arc day.

Making our way to the course during lunchtime on Sunday, it soon became apparent that this was an altogether different day than Saturday. All of Paris seemed to be descending on the racetrack and large queues were forming all around the course. Even though we were early, it quickly became evident that picking up the owners' badges was not going to be a straightforward process. Let's face it—this was not Sedgefield on a Thursday afternoon. Luckily our tour guide managed to get us through the massed queues and inside the racecourse, from which we attempted to locate the elusive badges. Given my very limited French and the number of people already milling about, it soon became obvious that obtaining the passes might be as tricky as Ribbons winning by ten lengths. However, my fellow Elite member, Gordon, had a cool head and mobile phone, which allowed us to access the Longchamp owners' reception office, where after some initial confusion, the owners' badges were indeed located. Inside the purple-coloured, Qatar-embossed pack was the Invitations Partants' card, with my name outlined, and below it that of Ribbons. One badge, it seems, does not suffice in France, and in total there were three multicolored badges we had to attach to navigate our way through the different parts of the "ring."

The first three races went by in a blur, until the moment itself arrived and I made my way down to the "ring" for the 3:45 p.m. race. To say that the ring was somewhat intimidating was an understatement. As I entered the ring through armed police and security officers, flashing the badges that enabled movement forward, I was suddenly aware of the hundreds of people looking down on us. There was a cacophony of noise, and in the crowd there were numerous

flags, particularly the Japanese ones (they had apparently been trying to win the Arc for many years and were there in force). Given all
the other ownership groups in attendance, it seemed to be a scene of
organised chaos. It was totally exciting.

My good fortune in obtaining the badge became clear to me as I
met up with my fellow Elite "owners." There were about eight of us,
and it seemed to me that only three were with my party. Most had
come over from the United Kingdom on the day of the race. Trying to
take it all in as it was happening before my eyes was some task, but
I maintained a watching brief. Claire Balding was there in her role as
Channel 4 anchor; she raced after various groups, with her camera
man trailing behind her. It amazed me that given Elite's prodigious
achievement of getting Ribbons there—to fly the flag, so to speak—,
that she didn't seem interested in speaking to us.

James Fanshawe appeared from the preparade area, and he seemed
to recognise who we were. Every inch the English Gent, he walked over
to meet us. Despite the high tension of the occasion, he was totally
courteous, shaking hands with everyone in the party and making some
general inquiries about how we had arrived in France. Understandably,
he appeared nervous as Ribbons paraded in front of us, although the
horse seemed at ease and a picture of equine health. We tentatively
asked James how Ribbons was and what her chances were. He reiter-
ated his earlier comments that he would have liked more rain. "But," he
said, "she's done all her homework." It wasn't a ringing endorsement,
but I felt that he thought she had a pretty good chance.

Suddenly, out of the melee in front of us appeared Frankie Dettori,
every inch the showman, with his arms theatrically raised above his
head, to avoid contact with the throngs of people who surrounded
us. The word "ebullient" was probably invented to describe the charismatic Italian jockey; he radiated positivity. Once more, he shook hands
with our party, and not surprisingly, he was upbeat about the horse's

chances. "I rode her in France last time," he said. "She's a very good horse." As Fanshawe and Dettori moved away from us to mount up, there appeared to be the usual final instructions between trainer and jockey. I always assume that this must have been decided well before that point, but it doesn't seem to vary, whether it's at Longchamp or Leicester; there always seems to be a final word. We presumed that the tactics would be to "hold her up" in the usual fashion and look for a late finish. With that, the ring began to empty, and we quickly made our way out among the crowd, looking for the best vantage point.

With my total focus on Ribbons, it was easy to forget the opposition, but this was a top-class race, and there were a host of dangers. As Ribbons paraded around, I noted with a little trepidation the horse just in front of her, Narniyn. Ridden by the crack French jockey Christophe Soumillon, it was among the fancied horses at 9–1. But the real reason for my fears was that the jockey was wearing my lucky colours—green and red! However, the more practical side of my betting head was reassured when I noted that Ribbons had beaten this horse at Deauville, but the going had been softer that day than the good going of today. The trainer John Gosden walked just in front of me as he helped William Buick onto the well-fancied Sultanina, a horse that had won the Nassau stakes at Goodwood. The British were well represented, and Roger Varian's listed winner, Hadatha, constituted yet another live danger. The biggest threat from the French horses appeared to be Freddy Head's We Are, a horse that had been controversially disqualified in one of her last races but shared second favouritism with Ribbons, at 6–1. The favourite for the race, though, was Dermot Weld's Tarfasha. She was at warm order at 3–1. Although she had been beaten in the Epsom and Irish Oaks, the tipsters felt her valiant efforts in those top-class races would see her come out on top on this day.

I had already placed a good few euros on Ribbons earlier in the afternoon, and although this was clearly going to be a tough race, it would appear that she had every chance.

Given the distance back to our pavilion stand, it was decided that it would make more sense to head for the main stand, nearest the parade ring. Rushing up the steps, we joined the largely French crowd that had thronged into this main stand. With a bit of bobbing and weaving, we arrived at a vantage point that gave a great view of the winning post.

• • •

THE RACE—PRIX DE L'OPERA (GROUP ONE), 3+ YEARS OLD, FILLIES/MARES, 1 MILE, 2 FURLONGS

We took our positions to see Ribbons make a good break from the stalls. I kept my binoculars trained on her, and she seemed to be settled and traveling well, but the horses were all going at a great lick. These were true thoroughbreds. They all seemed to be going at lightning speed, almost a blur to the naked eye. As they appeared at the top of the hill, they took a right-hand turn and set off for home with Nymphea in front, but all the other horses were queuing up behind her. The favourite, Tarfasha, was well positioned in third, and as they turned the final corner, she eased through to take the lead and seemingly was about to justify her favouritism. Keeping my binoculars trained on Ribbons, there seemed no doubt that she was traveling well in about fourth place, but she appeared to be boxed in.

Then it happened—one of those magical moments, probably exclusive to these top-class race events, Frankie spotted a gap, and as if pressing a button, Ribbons moved out to just behind the leader. Accelerating all the time, she took the lead with less than a hundred yards to go.

Scarcely able to believe my eyes and trying to keep calm as my pulse rate began to rocket, I started to mumble, "I don't believe it—we're going to win! Go on, Ribbons, you're going to do it!" Indeed, Ribbons maintained her momentum as Frankie drove her toward the finishing line. The favourite looked to be beaten, and victory seemed to be ours. However, all the horses were finishing as if in a flash, and no sooner had Ribbons hit the front than We Are flashed past on Ribbons's left to win by a neck.

So it was the French horse We Are that triumphed at odds of 6-1, with Ribbons at the same odds second, a neck ahead of Hadaatha, who finished third at odds of 9-1. Tarfasha, the 3-1 favourite for the race, finished fourth.

• • •

POSTRACE
Momentarily stunned by the result, I quickly regained my wits as we stumbled out of the grandstand and quickly made our way back to the ring. My emotions were scrambled, the initial disappointment of coming so close was quickly dissipated, after all Ribbons had run such a good race and we were now making our way toward the winner's enclosure. By coming second, Ribbons prize was €80,000.

The enclosure was just as hectic as before the race, if anything there were more people inside the ring now. The owners' group had reconvened and we appeared all equally delighted and slightly taken aback with the quality of Ribbons performance. We were not the only ones, James Fanshawe came toward us and was totally elated. He said, "Two furlongs out, I thought she was definitely going to win." At that point, Ribbons and Frankie appeared in our midst, all the group surrounded them and we all took the opportunity to pat and congratulate the horse. Frankie, ever the showman, cried mock tears as he prepared to dismount. "I reeeeally tried for you," he said. James kept repeating how pleased he was with Ribbons's performance, when to my right a French radio interviewer suddenly appeared and pushed a microphone toward James. "No!" he said. "I am not surprised by the horse's performance, and with a little more cut in the ground, she could have won. You don't get many fillies as good as this," he beamed.

With that, we were suddenly being ushered upstairs for the "complimentaries" that come with being in the winner's parade, as a gigantic escalator took us from the parade ring to the luxurious rooms above. I had been invited back to the odd glass of champagne in the course of the research for this book, but this was on an altogether different scale. At the top of the escalator, we were greeted by some young ladies, who ushered us into a large airy and opulent stand, where presumably "connections" were wined and dined. There were all sorts of luxurious sweets and savouries for us to consume, as we discussed Ribbons's bold efforts. As we patiently waited for our champagne to arrive, the news filtered through that they had actually run out of the stuff! Looking around and taking into account that this was the fourth race of the day, I began to realise why. This minor setback was not going to take the gloss off such a wonderful day, I toasted Ribbons in orange juice. *C'est la vie*, as the French say.

● ● ●

POSTSCRIPT—RIBBONS
Ribbons was kept in training for the 2015 flat season, as befitted her previous season's exploits; the five-year-old was targeted at top-class races only. On a mark of 114, she was undoubtedly the star of the Elite Club.

She started the season on the second day of the prestigious Dante meeting at York in a Group Two race of mares and fillies over one mile and two furlongs. I was at the Dante meeting, and although the "good" going wasn't ideal for Ribbons, she ran a respectable race and finished third. She seemed to travel well enough, and though initially four lengths off the pace, she finished with her usual flourish but was unable to catch the front two. James Fanshawe seemed pleased enough. It was a season opener, she had a three-pound penalty, and he was confident of her future prospects.

At the end of June, she appeared again, competing in the Pretty Polly stakes at the Curragh in Ireland. Over the same distance, this was a top-class Group One encounter featuring a couple of the season's top horses, Diamondsandrubies and Legatissimo. Reunited with Frankie Dettori, Ribbons put in a great performance, and in classic fashion, shot through the field late on. She was a narrow third in a blanket finish. The Nassau stakes was now mooted, but eventually this was swerved, and a decision was made to return to France to enable Ribbons to defend her title in the Jean Romanet. The return to Deauville didn't go according to plan. Ribbons seemed unusually keen at the start and didn't appear to settle over the first few furlongs. Pulling hard and farther up with the pace than usual, she was unable to finish in her usual style and came in sixth of the eleven horses (she was later promoted to fifth, following the disqualification of Bawina). Although this was a disappointing performance from Ribbons, it was put into context when one considered it was the first time in her career that she had finished outside the frame.

Any doubts that might have festered by this performance were quickly dispelled as Ribbons returned to winning ways in September, triumphing in the Blandford stakes back at the Curragh. This was more like the Ribbons of old, a classic holdup performance that saw her go from last to first in a blink of an eye and win the race in style. This was a classy performance by Ribbons, and it reinforced plans to enter her in the end-of-season showpiece, Champions Day at Ascot. But before that race would be run in October, the surprise news came through that Ribbons would be entered in the December Tattersall sale. Clearly aware of the commercial opportunities afforded by owning such a top-class horse, the "management" had decided to go to the sale, attempting to assuage any disgruntled members by stating that a substantial "reserve" would be set for the horse.

It was therefore a possibility that when Ribbons appeared at Ascot, it could be the last time she would race in the club's colours. The race was something of an anticlimax; Ribbons struggled to get into the contest and finished down the field, eighth in a field of thirteen. I wasn't really sure what to make of the "sale" news, I could see the economic arguments that would be involved in a sale, but at the same time I had developed an affinity with this horse that I had followed since she was a yearling. I had watched her develop into a top-class racehorse and one way or another had seen all her races. Now there was the distinct possibility that she would be sold. There was no question that she had turned out to be a star. I would always remember the joy she brought to all "connections" on that wonderful day at Longchamp. If she were to finish, her record was a wonderful testament to the Elite Racing Club and their breeding programme. In that sense I felt it was they who clearly had the right to make such an important decision and in that way I was happy to go along with it.

Ribbons finished the 2015 season at a crossroads. She headed to the sale a top-class horse. She had won six of her fourteen starts, only out of the places twice, and had amassed more than £350,000 in winnings. It was possible that the "reserve" would not be met and she might be retired to continue Elite's amazing achievements in the breeding line. Finally, it was also possible that in the case of the reserve not being met, she could race for the club again in the 2016 season.

When the sale came around in December, the "reserve" was not met, and the club decided to retire Ribbons to stud. So the club was true to its word. The horse was retained, and a new exciting chapter of the Elite breeding programme was begun. I, for one, was delighted. However, after the December sales it emerged that there had been a number of potential buyers who were still interested in the horse. In February 2016 the club announced that it had accepted an offer for Ribbons, consequently, Elite no longer owned her.

4
All Roads Lead To Carlisle

BRUNELLO WAS A horse that represented the polar opposite of the Stan Hey model of horse "ownership." Here was the cheapest possible option of purchasing a share in a racehorse. Therefore, under the concept of "ownership on a shoestring," it would meet the criteria I established at the outset. Namely, it would allow me to follow the horse's progress from training yard to racecourse and in due time obtain an ownership badge to see "my" horse run at a British racecourse. The "wheeze" to the plan, and the epitome of how it was going to differ from Stan Hey's experiences, was that it was going to cost nothing!

Brunello's ownership was syndicated by the appropriately named Own a Racehorse (OAR) organisation. From my admittedly non-comprehensive research, theirs was the cheapest way of "owning" a horse. At rock-bottom rates, it was possible to obtain a share in a horse for less than one hundred pounds. However, the real wheeze was that I noticed on their website that they offered the option of partial payment of such modest fees in Tesco vouchers. My wife, Sue, is an avid collector of such vouchers, and in the dim and distant past, I had pushed trolleys around the commercial giant. Instead of obtaining a toaster or a holiday, why not use a few of these vouchers to buy a share in Bruno (as he was affectionately known) Sue is a good sport, and with the recent experience of attending the race meetings outlined in this book, it took little persuasion for me to convince her of the soundness of the proposal. Because the majority of the cost was paid by Tesco vouchers, the amusing idea struck me that if Bruno managed to win any prize money, it might cover the "real" money I paid for the balance of the share. In such an eventuality and given the modest costs involved anyway, Brunello effectively cost nothing!

Thus, it came to pass that Bruno became the third horse in this "ownership" lark. He was hardly likely to be a Cheltenham prospect, but given his cost, I was intrigued to see where this "free" horse might take us. The OAR organisation had an excellent website, and I decided I would make this my most "virtual" ownership experience by dealing with information on their site and not make any e-mail or personal contact. However modest the cost, they seemed well organised, and although this was ownership on the thinnest of shoestrings, I was impressed with the specific information they forwarded. All the basics were covered; they gave me information about Bruno's previous travails and details about his trainer, Michael Smith. I knew little about the trainer other than the fact that he was young with a very small string based in Northumberland. Whenever a race was planned or the horse was declared to run, I would be sent quite detailed updates on his training, the nature of the race, and the calibre of the opposition.

I didn't expect very much from Bruno; he had been running in very low-grade races, his BHA mark was significantly lower than that of other horses I had seen, and life for him had been something of a struggle. When I took out my share in November 2014, he seemed to have run thirty-six times, winning once and being placed seven times. Rather worryingly, the solitary win had occurred more than two and a half years earlier, when running on the flat for David O'Meara. He had Kieren Fallon on board that day and went off odds-on, but that was now a distant memory. Now he ran in Class Five races in some sort of Trivial Pursuit of winning, but of course enabling a syndicate to watch him at the races. He seemed to have been with the OAR organisation for some time, with another one of its trainers, Tom Gratton, unable to coax an elusive victory out of him. He was hurdling now, but he still wasn't likely to run in any "good" races and appeared even less likely to win any of them.

Nonetheless, something appealed to me about the horse and his situation. Despite his long run without success, he seemed to have built up a loyal band of supporters, who I assumed had been shareholders through this barren period. I had read somewhere that the majority of horse owners don't actually see their horses win very often, if at all. Indeed, Mr. Hey's horses did just that, at great expense. I tried to analyse the situation with a little logic, knowing full well that logic appears to have little to do with the thrill of ownership. Clearly, Bruno was a very limited horse that had not "made it" on the flat and had not made any significant improvement over hurdles. However, I told myself, he was still only six, and under Michael Smith, he was going to go chasing. He was built like a chaser, although he clearly wasn't fast; maybe he could jump. I had bought the share just as Bruno was about to start life as a chaser. Maybe a new page would be turned.

It was not an auspicious start to Bruno's chasing career later in November, when he was pulled up in bog-like conditions at Hexham. Bruno really struggled, losing two shoes in the mud. Later it was rather superfluously reported that the horse didn't like the conditions and that in the future, "good" would need to feature somewhere in the going description. I considered that might be a difficult requirement while running these North country tracks in winter.

It was therefore with little sense of optimism that I set up my computer to watch Bruno's second attempt over the big obstacles, when he ran at Catterick over the festive period. This was a Class

Five two-mile, three-furlong chase, and not much was expected of Bruno; he was seventh of the nine horses in the betting. It might be Christmas, I thought, but a certain amount of pragmatism was called for. I decided on a modest £2.50 each-way bet, at odds of 12–1.

Although what followed was not likely to feature in an edited highlight package of the jumps season, it was, in its own way, quite remarkable. Bruno set off well and was soon leading, jumping really fluently as he led the horses around the first circuit. I began to perk up because on the next circuit, he showed little sign of weakening. Approaching the last two fences, he retained the lead, although the two cofavourites were closing the gap behind him. The expected outcome seemed imminent as Moonlight Maggie drew up to Bruno and then smoothly went past him as they jumped the last. Well, he had given it a good go, and I was consoling myself with the each-way bet when Adam Nichol somehow cajoled a further effort out of the horse. Before my disbelieving eyes, Bruno rallied, and with the line in sight, he swept past the favourite to win! What a performance! Bruno had revealed a depth of spirit rarely spotted previously in his runs. In what was his second race for me, so to speak, he had recorded his first win in thirty-three months. He had won prize money of more than £3000, and of course I had my winning bet. The "free horse" strategy had paid off already.

I couldn't help noting the irony of the moment. Here was a horse that had never set the world alight jumping like the proverbial stag, whereas Doyly Carte, a winner at Cheltenham, was failing over the large obstacles and had fallen at this very track earlier in the month.

The handicapper took note of the improvement and moved Bruno up from the depths of a mark of 90 to a figure of 99. In horse racing, you do not get long to savour the moment. I waited to see if this new standard was to be maintained in Bruno's next races. His next race at

Musselburgh was a step up to Class Four standard. Bruno, jumping well, again led the field, but this time he was caught, finishing sixth of nine. He stayed in a Class Four race as he returned to the scene of his triumph, Catterick. In typical fashion, Bruno took the other four horses around a circuit and boldly tried to stay with the hot favourite, but in the end, he had to settle for third place. However, he was in the money again; the princely sum of £763 was recorded.

April brought a return to Class Five company as connections sought out a good winning opportunity. Bruno ran in another two-mile, four-furlong handicap at Sedgefield. I still hadn't seen Bruno run and was being a little blasé about obtaining this owner's badge. Something always seemed to get in the way—either a family booking or being out of the country. This was Easter Sunday, but I sneaked off to the computer to see if he could return to winning ways. But with Bruno being the seventh favourite of the thirteen runners, a place seemed his best chance. *Timeform* neatly summed up his chasing career thus far by saying, "Improved upon poor chasing debut when game winner at Catterick...not quite in same form in either subsequent appearance, but still enters calculations."

Despite a strong favourite, I decided on a tenner straight win. Bruno seemed happy enough as he bowled along, jumping well. He took the lead four out and led up to the tenth fence, but then, despite a slight rally, he was beaten and finished in fourth place.

It was another gutsy run. Bruno was definitely a wholehearted animal that was giving us a run for our money. As is the nature of handicap racing, his mark was now dropping. At 95, it was just three pounds above his winning mark. I was determined that whatever happened in the next race I would put in for an owner's badge to see this likeable horse. However, all of April passed with no further declarations. I was just beginning to think I had left it too late when news filtered through that Bruno would be declared to run at Carlisle on May 7, General Election day. I was a little disappointed that with the season at its end, Bruno was back hurdling, but this was tempered by the fact that the race would be at Carlisle, one of my favourite courses. My ownership application was successful. The next day, we set off to Carlisle to see Bruno run in a two-mile, three-furlong handicap hurdle.

• • •

RACE DAY—BRUNELLO AT CARLISLE, THURSDAY, MAY 7, 2015
THE RACECOURSE

Carlisle is one of my favourite courses in Britain. We had been dragging the kids there for years when they were young, and we holidayed in the Lake District. It had remained a fixture for my wife and me, and we attended races there five or six times a year. Recently we had been able to target Britain's oldest race the Carlisle Bell and the Cumberland Plate races. It was an archetypal country course located in the pleasant countryside of Blackwell village, just outside Carlisle. Although both codes of flat and jumps racing are practiced here, it has the feel of a jumps course. The fences are a stiff test, and I have noticed that the top trainers often send their chasing hopes there at the season's start, as some form of pipe opener. However, Bruno's aptitude in that capacity was not to be tested on this day; he was returning to timber.

The key feature of the track is a stiff uphill finish; horses clearly need stamina around here, particularly in the mud of winter. That was not likely to be a factor on this day, though, because this was the final jumps meeting of the season, on a lovely early summer evening.

The owners' and trainers' facilities at Carlisle are excellent. Owners of all description are given a very warm welcome by helpful attendants and pointed in the direction of the owners' and trainers' bar area, underneath the old main stand, which is head-on to the finish line. There is a bust displayed outside this modernised facility of legendary local trainer Gordon Richards. Inside, his son, Nicky, was talking with some owners. The complimentaries were there in abundance, with the usual tea and biscuits, along with an excellent homemade pie. Mind you, I had to gulp it down quickly because Bruno was featured in the opening race.

• • •

PRERACE
I wandered down to the preparade ring where Bruno was being saddled up and quickly acquainted myself with the OAR members. As with all other syndicate owners I had met over the past seventeen months, they seemed to be eminently sensible racing folk who clearly had a soft spot for "our" Bruno. He had gathered a bit of a following; some of the members had clearly been with him for some time. Maybe it was that experience that urged caution. Not too many appeared fully confident regarding his chances; they had been encouraged by his chasing exploits. But like me, they were a little mystified as to why he was hurdling.

Once in the ring, we met up with trainer Michael Smith, a pleasant chap who involved himself in the usual small talk that precedes a race. Like nearly every other trainer I had met, regardless of the quality of the race, he seemed a little apprehensive, unsure about what was going to happen in the race. I noted that the *Racing Post* stats had him 0 from 12 at Carlisle, so clearly this wasn't his lucky course. But I reasoned that, given the nature of his string, he was not likely to have had too many "live" chances. He was a local trainer trying to make a living in a tough business. One thing was certain: he had already done a great job with Bruno. Adam Nichol, whose brilliant ride at Catterick was largely responsible for Bruno's breathtaking win, now appeared, doffing his cap to all present.

This was a conditional jockeys' race, which I gathered was for jockeys who were apprentices in NH terms, usually under the age of twenty-six and with less than seventy-five winners in their career thus far. Adam was clearly a very promising jockey. Just across from us was Nico de Boinville, who earlier in the year had won the Cheltenham Gold Cup on Coneygree. As always, jockey and trainer moved away for a last-minute word about tactics. I assumed that Bruno would be once more employing his front-running tactics and maybe run the race out of some of his competitors before that stiff finish.

This was a Class Four race; that did not shout out quality. And Bruno was halfway down the weights and further still in the betting. The McManus colours were in the opposition, along with a fancied McCain horse, and the local Indepub was a slight favourite in an open-looking contest.

I was absolutely delighted to be there on such a lovely evening, but I was less than confident about "our" horse's chances. I had no trouble finding 12–1, and I hedged my bet, going each way in the hope that he would run to a place. The racing press, though, seemed to think he had a chance. *Timeform*, in its usual dry manner, noted his gutsy win at Catterick and implied that he had run similarly good races since, clearly leaving us to make up our own minds as to how he would do on this day. The *Racing Post* was more upbeat; their writer considered that his last hurdle performance when fourth at Wetherby was good enough to put him on their short list. As the horses made their way out of the ring, we all moved up the stairs in the old grandstand, which gives a great view out over the picturesque course. I had noted in the past that although this is the older stand, its location is still favoured by the trainers, presumably because of the view and close access to the parade ring. There I was on the gantry, looking down on my own horse, as Bruno ran down to the start.

• • •

THE RACE—HANDICAP HURDLE (CLASS 4) 2 MILES, 3 FURLONGS
The race was something of an anticlimax, as Bruno looked jaded and was never really in the contest. He started reasonably soundly, and as I trained the binocs on him, I thought his jumping looked as clean as ever. However, fatigue possibly seemed to affect him as the contest went on. What was clear to me was that Bruno was certainly not moving with any great speed between the obstacles, and instead of building up the optimism with that lung-bursting front running, he seemed content to be tucked in behind the leaders. With one circuit gone, the front runners began to stretch the field, which became increasingly strung out.

My hopes that Bruno was saving something up for the stiff finish were quickly dashed as he dropped farther behind and, if anything, was now going slower between the obstacles. Eventually Tara Mac broke away to win comfortably eight lengths ahead of the McCain horse, with Parles Pond coming in third. It really was quite a procession as the other horses finished with some big gaps between them. Bruno eventually finished sixth, over twenty lengths behind the winner. Although Bruno was over thirty lengths ahead of the pre race favourite, Indepub, who trailed in ninth and last of the finishers.

• • •

POSTRACE

We quickly made our way to the preparade area, where Adam was dismounting after the race. There didn't appear to be much time for any sort of detailed debrief. The consensus appeared to be that Bruno didn't have much left in the locker, was tired, and had run accordingly. Some mentioned how happy they were that he was back safe and sound. I have found that this is a very common refrain from certain owners at the end of races. They really do seem to care for their horses and seem to be almost in a state of tension when the horse runs. I had seen enough in this project to know that much worse things can happen to horses than running down the field. I returned to the owners' building, where I ran into a couple of fellow owners who had followed Bruno for some time. They seemed reasonably satisfied. The consensus was that he had run a bit "flat" but had done OK this season. I was totally enjoying the occasion and was relatively sanguine regarding the race's outcome. Bruno, it seemed to me, was a big, honest horse that could jump a fence. He was never going to grace jumping's showcase events, but really that was irrelevant. He was destined to run in low-grade jumps races in the North, and as long as he gave his best, his supporters and connections would be satisfied. In my little research project, he had been the "free" horse, and I was delighted with his efforts. It could be that he would develop a little further over the big obstacles as he gained more experience, and he might just delight his connections by winning another race. He was the "free" horse in my string, that even brought in a little money as the sum of nine pounds was returned to my account! More importantly, he and OAR had given me a great day out at one of my favourite racecourses. For that and his unbelievable finish at Catterick, I'll always remember Brunello.

• • •

POST SCRIPT—BRUNELLO

Brunello was put away for the summer and was to continue his chasing career in October 2015. Loyalty and appreciation of the seven-year-old gelding's performances dictated that I take out another year's share in Bruno. This time I paid in "real" money, using the winnings as a small part payment.

When October came around, Bruno was apparently fit and raring to go. In a surprise move, Michael Smith decided to give him a first run in a flat race over one mile, seven furlong at Catterick. This apparently was merely to give him a run and blow away the cobwebs. Bruno came in last of the nine runners. Bruno's next appearance was back in a chase over a distance of three miles at Wetherby. He appeared to be back in his old front-running style, jumping his fences cleanly and seemingly going well. It was therefore something of a shock that when he reached the ninth fence he decided to bypass it and unseated his rider in the process! This was a somewhat bizarre outcome to a race in which he had appeared to be going well. Undeterred, within ten days he was declared at Sedgefield to run over a marathon three mile and two furlongs. Bruno was never going well under the heavy conditions, managing to lose a shoe before being pulled up after the fourteenth fence.

It was all so resonant of twelve months before when Bruno pulled up in the mud at Hexham, minus two shoes! Of course he followed that race by winning in style. For Bruno and his supporters, tomorrow is always another day.

5
All Roads Lead To Bangor and Cartmel

CHILLY MISS WAS a filly syndicated through the Racegoers Club, owned by the Racecourse Association, which proudly proclaims that it is a club that promotes "racegoing and a greater involvement in the sport." In existence since 1968 and with a main function of encouraging the public to attend race days, I also noted upon joining that it also ran small horse-owning syndicates. The not-for-profit organisation seemed to be promoting a good product. I quickly realised that by attending a few discounted meetings, the discounts would pay for the subscription. I was so impressed that I got my wife to join. After all, this ownership research project had involved her in a good deal of paparazzi activity already. Almost by chance, I realised that as a member, I was entitled to join one of their horse ownership syndicates for a modest payment of £225 (which gave me a 0.5 percent share in the horse). Although this hardly propelled me into the blue-blood league of owners, it was my biggest venture in the shoestring ownership caper.

This syndicate was much smaller, with just two hundred shares per horse. Once more, this entitled the shareholder to regular bulletins about the horse and the prospect of appearances in the owner's ring on race days. The club appeared to offer two horses—one in the North and one in the South—given my location the Northern horse was plumped for. The other factor in this choice that appealed was that this horse was advertised as a dual-purpose horse. Given my preference for watching the jumping, it appealed to me that this horse would go summer jumping, in addition to any flat races it ran in. The horse was trained by Malcolm Jefferson, and his daughter, Ruth, at Norton in North Yorkshire. Although this would mean having to take out all sorts of inoculations to travel from the right side of the Pennines to the self-proclaimed God's own country of Yorkshire, the horse's CV looked good enough to take that chance.

Malcolm was an experienced trainer, with some impressive wins at Cheltenham in the past, and an owner's visit to the stables left one impressed with the quality of the training operation. We all escorted the trainers to watch Chilly on the gallops. Although it was difficult to take much from this brief excursion, there did appear to be a good deal of confidence in the filly, from both the Jefferson team and fellow syndicate members. A good deal of this confidence was derived from the fact that in the previous season, Chilly had won her first two races. Both were bumper races, and Chilly had excited her connections, particularly in the second race, where the filly had beaten an odds-on shot, ridden by a certain Tony McCoy. After that, carrying more weight and occasionally racing against the boys, it got a bit harder for Chilly, but she was clearly a resilient horse, often making the frame. Being dual purpose, she had also raced on the flat, and her best performance had been a third at a big meeting at Newcastle. Although my primary interest was in the jumps, the dual-purpose factor appealed to me, not least because of the prospect of watching some jumps with the sun on our backs. Deep down, I was hoping that Chilly would prove to be a good hurdler; it was what the Jeffersons excelled at. But if there were some sun-filled days on the flat to contend with, I'm sure I could take that on board!

The Racegoers Club proved adept at communications, and from March 2015 onward, I got regular e-mail updates on the horse's training progress via the ever-helpful Kelly. Initial vibes from the Jeffersons were very positive. The filly was well regarded, and the previous year's efforts had galvanised hopes that the horse could become a useful performer. Early e-mails were littered with this optimism, Chilly was working well and showing a good appetite for her work.

The initial plan was to start over the flat, apparently to take advantage of what was considered a "workable handicap mark." Accordingly, a one-mile, two-furlong handicap race was chosen at Doncaster. This race seemed to be considered something of an outing, to see how she would get on after her break. "Let's see what happens" seemed to be the main prerace vibe. What did happen was that Chilly came in seventh of fifteen runners. The *Racing Post* asserted that Chilly "dwelt behind, was pushed along, making headway three furlongs out, one pace." The Racegoers Club seemed satisfied, commenting that Chilly had run a "highly respectable" race. Within eleven days, Chilly was turned out again, presumably still trying to take advantage of her handicap mark. This time, Catterick was the venue, and Chilly was declared to run in a one-mile, five-furlong handicap. Optimism in the camp appeared to know no bounds, Malcolm was reported to be "really happy" and "as confident as I can be about Chilly." With the *Racing Post* tipping our filly, surely this was the moment to join the Harry Findlays of this world by placing the proverbial "mortgage" on such a good thing. In the event, the more Presbyterian elements in my nature came to the fore, and I placed a modest tenner on the filly to win. Of the twelve runners that went to post, Chilly finished seventh. The succinct *Racing Post* commentary read, "Slowly into stride, toward rear, ridden four furlongs out, never dangerous." Watching the race at the bookies, I had to concur. There was no getting away from it; this was a disappointing show, and the connections seemed confounded. The only upshot of this tame display was that the flat-racing plans seemed to be jettisoned. News soon came through that Chilly would be schooled to start hurdling, with a possible outing the next month at Sedgefield.

There now followed mixed messages regarding Chilly's innate ability at hurdling. First reports were that she was "a natural," But she wasn't declared for Sedgefield because it was decided that she needed more practice. Such foibles were ironed out, and Chilly made her hurdling debut at Wetherby in May. It was a two-mile maiden hurdle, and with top Northern jockey Brian Hughes on board, there was cautious optimism that, at the very least, Chilly would achieve a "clear round of jumping." This she achieved, but little else in a disappointing run, finishing fifth of seven, behind Philip Hobbs's odds-on horse. Although there was little shame in this, I was a little concerned that she trailed in behind 50-1 and 20–1 shots.

For Chilly and the "connections," these were worrying times. Her impressive bumper form was fading from memory, and Malcolm confessed that he was "very disappointed" and unable to explain the latest poor showing. As with everything in life, all things are relative, and although there was a downbeat feel to Chilly's progress, the connections of the fancied second favorite, Soeur De Rois, had more serious things to contemplate as their horse suffered a fatal injury.

Chilly, though, was proving to be a tough customer and an ideal syndicate horse because just twelve days later, she was declared to run in another two-mile novice hurdle, this time at Southwell. Relief was felt all around because this time, Chilly ran well, and although she was beaten by a "good one," Chilly keep going to make the frame.

Her third place put the syndicate in the money, with a prize of £477 claimed!

Optimism was now in the air, Ruth's schooling reports were very encouraging, and the filly was learning the game and pleasing everyone. The picturesque Lake District course of Cartmel was Chilly's next venue, where at the end of June she took part in a two-mile, one-furlong handicap hurdle. Although she ran into a Gordon Elliot "hot pot" that ran away with the race, Chilly showed commendable spirit to plug away and grab second place. The prize money was pouring in now, with £859 pocketed! Chilly was making progress, indeed taking into account the horse's performances the previous year in National Hunt races, it could now be claimed that in Chilly's last six races in this code, she had been placed in five. This last race had been significant—with it being the horse's third hurdle race, she would now be allocated an official handicap rating, which would determine the weight she would carry in a handicap race. Chilly was proving to be a fair horse with prospects, but would the handicapper saddle her with too much weight?

In the event, the horse received an official mark of 108, a modest mark, but one that could be considered a starting point. On the stable visit, Malcolm pronounced the mark a "fair" one; Ruth seemed less sure. The decision was quickly made that Chilly would make her handicap bow back at Cartmel in three weeks. The Jeffersons seemed to have placed the horse well—"It's in a lovely small field" was how Kelly described the six horses that were declared for the two-mile mares' handicap hurdle.

On the day of the race, the horse was described as being in "good order." In a strange coincidence, the Elite race-tipping service napped the filly. This time, my tenner was placed with a fair amount of confidence, despite Chilly being available at a generous 4–1 and drifting to 9–2 before the off. Such confidence was rewarded as Chilly romped home. In their usual concise and unemotional three-liner, the *Racing Post* summarised that Chilly was "held up in fourth, headway into second between the last two, effort last, soon ridden, stayed on to lead final 120 yards." It could have been the shipping forecast! But it was a red-letter day for "connections" and a syndicated horse winner. Ruth Jefferson was reportedly delighted with Chilly's efforts, and there was a noticeably polished ride from Brian, who timed his challenge to perfection. An elated Kelly e-mailed the pleasing feedback, and the prize money was now in the thousands, albeit £3899. Success can come at a cost, though, and in this case, with Chilly winning she would now be allocated more weight for her next race. The BHA decided to increase the mark from 108 to 115, which meant that our tough little filly would have to shoulder an extra burden of seven pounds. Of course this is the nature of handicap racing. Would the extra penalty stop Chilly's upward curve, or would the horse prove to be good enough to go up another notch?

I decided that this was the moment to go into the owner's ring and watch Chilly Miss in her next race. The Racegoers Club is a democratic operation, and they allocate owners' badges in a drawn rotation to different members. Circumstances had stymied some earlier plans to see the horse. Now, with July nearly over, I successfully entered the draw and obtained my badge to see Chilly run at the Bangor on Dee racecourse.

• • •

RACE DAY—CHILLY MISS AT BANGOR ON DEE, FRIDAY, JULY 31, 2015
THE RACECOURSE
Bangor on Dee racecourse in North Wales seemed to me to be quite unique. I had heard course specialist Donald McCain say on a stable visit that it was the last place you would expect to locate a racecourse. The bare course statistics, as outlined in the programme do little to

convey the quirky nature of this course. The programme describes a "left-handed track" with "nine relatively easy fences," emphasising the "three tight turns" that characterise the sharp nature of the course. Basically, the course is located down in a bowl-shaped depression, and amazingly had no grandstand. Ownership perks, it seemed, were to be limited on this day! Once the horses had left the parade ring and gone down to the start, the crowd stood on the top of the hill and watched the horses running in the basin below.

My reception for the owner's badge at the kiosk, although far from the frosty jobsworths that amusingly confronted Stan Hey, was, shall we say, perfunctory.

On enquiry about the location and availability of owner's facilities, I was told to follow my nose around the corner from the entrance, where in front of the preparade area stood a small owners' and trainers' bar. The privileged freebies seemed sparse—they did not even offer a biscuit to dip into the complimentary tea. Given my previous experiences, I mentally downgraded the North Welsh course. Gripping my complimentary programme, I noted that Chilly was fancied. *Timeform* opined that she "merited respect" and tipped the filly to win.

• • •

PRERACE

The syndicate members, about a dozen in all, met in the parade ring, where Ruth Jefferson came to meet us. Chilly's recent win had buoyed spirits within the syndicate, but they seemed a knowledgeable bunch and were conscious of the extra weight Chilly had to carry. The previous week's wet weather had been something of a concern as Chilly did not like it soft, but on the day of the race, the weather was warm and the going good. Ruth was pleasant and outgoing, although a little hesitant about Chilly's chance. "Let's wait and see" seemed to be the general consensus. Brian Hughes courteously shook hands with all syndicate members and claimed he would keep Chilly "handy" In the race, by which I think he meant up with the front runners.

It was noticeable, as on all my other race days, that syndicate parties in the ring always dwarf the number of owners with other horses; occasionally the trainer and jockey can be totally on their own. I liked to think that our enthusiastic number offer a welcome stimulant, not a distraction, to the trainer and jockey.

Chilly paraded around the ring calmly enough, although some thought she seemed a little agitated. Possibly she was aware that the *Racing Post* had napped her to win the race. However, the RGC excellent prerace assessment left no doubt that this was a tough assignment for Chilly. She had Richard Johnson's and Sam Twiston-Davies's noticeable bookings, the experienced workbench, and a number of dangerous Irish raiders to contend with. Undaunted, I marched to the bookies to place my twenty-pound-win bet, having no trouble getting 6–1. Money did appear to be coming in for our filly as she started as the second favourite at 5–1, but to me this looked an open race.

• • •

THE RACE—HANDICAP HURDLE (CLASS 4) 2 MILES, 3 FURLONGS
The concise *Racing Post* summary said, "Took keen hold, prominent challenged three out until before next, no extra." This was a fair reflection on what was a disappointing run from the filly. My view from the hill was that she seemed a little too keen early in the race and was pulling a little. She seemed comfortable with the pace, and as Brian had said, was up with the front runners. However, when it came to the business end of the race and the other horses began to accelerate, Chilly was left in their slip stream. Chebsey

Beau was the surprise winner of the race at the juicy odds of 18-1. Charlie Longsden's Java Rose was a clear second, with Workbench in third place. The next horses finished in quite close order with Chilly finishing in seventh place of the thirteen runner field. When a horse doesn't make the frame, it is usually a question of quickly trying to locate the jockey and trainer before they disappear. However, in this case this was not a problem, as our horse was brought back into the rear of the parade ring where Brian, Ruth, and the syndicate gathered. Brian was short and to the point. He said Chilly had "pulled too hard at the start" and that it seemed had done for her chances. He indicated that he had eased down on the run in. "I wasn't hard on her," he said. A possible mitigating factor was that Chilly had taken a kick at the start that caused a cut in her back leg. Again the fickle nature of fate came to the fore, as it was subsequently found to have just missed an artery. Ruth, clearly disappointed, was wondering about Chilly's gears, as she had clearly been caught short when the others accelerated. Here was a trainer who really cared. Amazingly, she stood talking it through with us for fully twenty minutes. By the time we were forced to vacate the parade thing, for the horses to parade before the next race, Ruth's spirits were restored, and the race was more valuable experience for our durable little filly.

$$\bullet \quad \bullet \quad \bullet$$

POST RACE

Given the positive vibes before the race, not least from the trade papers, there was an air of disappointment for Chilly's connections postrace. As always, a common syndicate comment relating to the safety and well-being of the animal was widely voiced. To me, the extra weight must have been a factor in the horse's performance, but now discussion turned to tactics and distance. The relationship between jockey and trainer is always a vital one in any horse's performance.

Ruth seemed to wonder whether Chilly would benefit from being "dropped out" a little in races—not racing too near the front.

One thing all agreed on was that Chilly was proving to be an ideal syndicate horse, Ruth opined that she got fat if she wasn't racing, and the seven races already run during the summer suggested that obesity was not going to be an option. An eighth race was quickly announced, with Chilly to return to the site of her victory, Cartmel.

Now, of course, the concept behind this book is to be owner for the day once, for five different horses. However, with the news that Chilly was to run again at one of my favourite courses, I felt that I could tweak my own rules. Luckily, I obtained an owner's badge for the Cartmel meeting, on the August bank holiday weekend.

Amazingly, one of Elite's horses, Volcanic (also trained by Donald McCain) was also running on the same card. Surely this was too good an opportunity to miss. To be owner for the day for two horses would surely have made Stan Hey eat his heart out!

And so it was down to the ever-picturesque Cartmel course for the meeting on a sunny August Saturday. Soon we would see if Chilly could put her Bangor disappointment behind her and, at the same time, see if Volcanic could achieve a first "chase" win.

• • •

RACE DAY—CHILLY MISS AT CARTMEL, SATURDAY, AUGUST 29, 2015
THE RACECOURSE
The racecourse is located in the shadow of the twelfth-century priory. This, together with the picture-book Cumbrian landscape, surely

make it one of England's most beautiful race-course settings. For the August Bank Holiday weekend meeting, all of the traditional fairground activities and stalls were in full swing, located in the centre of the course. It's a flat track of one mile, one furlong in circumference. The six fences are not the stiffest, but the longest run in of any British National Hunt course is more of a test; horses need to concentrate and have something left in the tank.

Having previously always watched all my races from the fairground centre having my ownership badge on this occasion meant I could watch the races from their one grandstand, suitably constructed of Lake District stone. This was definitely a step up from the restricted central view, with the grandstand affording a good perspective of the track, with only the far corner of the course obscured.

Cartmel is one of Britain's summer jumping courses, and by definition, National Hunt is a winter sport, so the better horses are rested in the summer months. Therefore, one would not expect the field to be on a fast track to Cheltenham, but there is no doubt that the Cumbrian course has been attracting better fields in more recent years.

There was nothing second class about the owners' facilities, which were excellent. From the two jolly ladies at the reception desk right through to the marquee that housed the owners' and trainers' facilities, one was met by good cheer. In line with the many local craft products found throughout the enclosure, the owners' tent would have gladdened the heart of any Enid Blyton readers, with literally lashings of tea and coffee and a great variety and profusion of homemade cakes. In addition to this, a ramble around the enclosure allowed us to purchase the appropriately named Hurdler real ale and pots of Morecambe Bay shrimp.

Suitably refreshed, we made our way down to the parade ring to meet Ruth, Brian, and the rest of the syndicate.

• • •

PRERACE

Many familiar faces of the syndicate were present in the parade ring, but what was noticeable this time was that Chilly was saddled up late and went to the start after just one lap of the parade ring. Ruth explained that this was a precaution to prevent the filly from getting agitated, as this may have been a reason for her pulling hard in her previous race.

This was clearly a better quality race for Chilly. It was the feature race on the card, the Cartmel Cup, a Class Three event. Chilly seemed feasibly handicapped, carrying five pounds less than at Bangor, and my fellow owners were encouraged by her winning form at this quirky track. The official message from RGC was that Malcolm was upbeat, thinking the horse had a good chance, and that he didn't think there was much between the horses in this contest. Once more on race day, it was Ruth who was in the ring, and she appeared quieter as she discussed tactics with Brian. The jockey told us he would keep Chilly "handy" as we cheerfully bade him good luck.

This seemed to be a tougher race. Chebsey Beau, who had beaten Chilly at Bangor, was in the lineup, and there was a profusion of threatening locally trained horses from the stables of James Moffatt and Martin Toddhunter.

Although delighted to be there and totally enjoying the Cumbrian ambience, I was less convinced of Chilly's chances. Loyalty dictated the placing of the twenty-pound wager, but I sought out the each-way bet and had no trouble getting on at 8–1.

The *Racing Post*, so bullish on our filly's chances at Bangor, now opined that she could have been "undone by the higher mark" at Bangor, and "more" would be needed now.

• • •

THE RACE—HANDICAP HURDLE (CLASS FOUR) 2 MILES, 3 FURLONGS

More was indeed needed, but unfortunately a tired-looking Chilly failed to oblige.

Chilly seemed more settled in the race and was always with the pacesetters until the "business end" of the race, when once more Chilly seemed to stay in the same gear as the main protagonists raced away to fight out the finish. The local horses did well with James Moffatt's Captain Brown winning the race and the Todd-Hunter horse Miss Macnamara coming third. Chebsey Beau, who had won impressively at Bangor, ran another good race to come second. It was a tired-looking Chilly that hauled herself up that long Cartmel finish, to grab fifth place. There were only two other finishers, who appeared to come in ages after our filly, and two other horses gave up the ghost, being pulled up and unseating the rider. The *Racing Post*, as always dry and to the point, recorded Chilly as "Chased leaders, not fluent first, weakened, after last."

• • •

POSTRACE

This time the race debrief was conducted on the course, as most of the syndicate raced over to hear Ruth's and Brian's thoughts. Ruth was as open and informative as ever. Although a little disappointed, she praised the horse's resilience. and when I asked was that likely to be it for the summer season, she quickly replied, "Definitely not."

There were other options and other days to be had, or so it seemed. Brian was similarly upbeat. He said, the horse was a great trier, had not been out of her depth in a Group Three race, and would win again. Such was the nature of the racing game. it seemed, The horse was safe and sound, was learning, and lived to fight another day.

The Racegoers Club's e-mail some days later was a little more cautious about Chilly. Now there was some comment on Chilly's tired and laboured finish. Nonetheless, the plan seemed to be to get a couple more races in, if possible, with a race at Perth being mentioned in dispatches.

• • •

POSTSCRIPT—CARTMEL

As mentioned earlier, I was doubly blessed at Cartmel because one of Elite's horses, Volcanic, was running on the same card. So I was lucky enough to be "owner" of two horses that day, and I had the opportunity to see if Donald McCain's novice chaser could claim a first win over the "big" fences.

Volcanic was that relatively rare Elite horse—it had been bought and was therefore not a homebred. It takes a lot longer to breed and race a National Hunt horse, and with retirements decimating Elite's jumpers, the management seemed to have listened to members like me who had long called for some new blood. Volcanic arrived from France, with some wins in that country, and it was hoped that he had the potential to succeed here. I had seen him hurdling a couple of times, including a perfunctory win at Carlisle, where he seemed to have run twice the distance of the other horses because he was jumping so far out to his left! I also enjoyed a marvelous trip to Aintree (where the owners' facilities and perks were second to none), but Volcanic struggled that day and had to pull up.

Although nothing out of the ordinary, Donald McCain had teased three hurdle wins out of the horse, and the plan now was to go novice chasing. McCain appeared a clever trainer at placing the horse, but so far no chase wins had been recorded, and as the Cartmel programme commented, Volcanic "has had his fair share of chances."

However, it seemed to me that he was in a much more winnable race than Chilly was to encounter. He was one of just six horses that lined up for the Class Four beginners' chase over two miles, five furlongs. With experienced jockey Wayne Hutchinson on board, it was a different syndicate of owners that crowded around him to assess the favourite's chances. The horse had failed spectacularly when 4–5 on at Cartmel in June, coming in third in a four- horse race, but Wayne seemed comfortable with favouritism.

Once the race was underway, Volcanic showed a good appetite for the fences and galloped around the course enthusiastically, soon taking the lead and staying well up the demanding finish to win by eight lengths. There is no doubt that it is one of life's pleasures to have "your" horse running around one of your favorite tracks, but it's even nicer when he wins! The proud owners were elated. One of them said, "I always thought he was a good 'un," although the horse's indifferent recent form had probably put him on the sell list. All that was forgotten now as the horse was patted down and Wayne was congratulated on his stylish ride. And although Mr. McCain was absent, his head lad seemed suitably chuffed. All the owners could just fit onto the winners' stand for the photographs, while the nominated spokesperson went up to collect the Cartmel sticky toffee pudding!

At this point, one of the course officials made his way over to us, congratulating all and inviting us into the winners' marquee for a glass of champagne and a playback of the race. The marquee was moderately busy, and unlike in Paris, the champagne had not run out!

With the champers, we enjoyed a bowl of cherries while we watched Volcanic's comfortable win again. Cartmel certainly knew how to treat its winning owners! At this point, Lord Cavendish, chairman of the course and owner of the nearby Holker Hall, wandered over to add his congratulations.

Looking like a character out of a Bertie Wooster novel, beaming, he leaned across to me and asked, "Had many winners at Cartmel in the past?"

After a long pause, I replied, "Not recently."

• • •

POSTSCRIPT—CHILLY MISS

Chilly Miss didn't make the race at Perth in September. Just a few days after that e-mail, news came through that she had sustained a niggling back injury. Although it was considered minor, it was showing up in her training, so the sensible decision was made to call it a day for the season.

Chilly had proved to be the ideal syndicate horse, tough and durable; she had run eight times that summer. With one win and two places, she could be considered to have had a successful time of it. Certainly I was pleased with her. She hadn't been able to take advantage of her flat handicap mark but had registered some pleasing hurdle runs and had achieved a modest but satisfactory BHA mark.

At six, she clearly held some promise for the future, and Ruth talked of establishing a new owners' group for the summer of 2016.

We were told that accounts would be settled for the existing group within a month. I put my bankers on standby!.

6
All Roads Lead Nowhere

GEOLOGY WAS ALSO a horse from the Elite Racing Club string. Again, it was breeding that interested me and was the factor in nominating him as my last "ownership" research horse. However, it wasn't the breeding on the Elite side that interested me; the Elite dam had been the well-regarded Baralinka. It was the sire that grabbed my attention; he was the famous Rock of Gibraltar. Elite, it seemed, had always put a premium on sending its broodmares to high-class stallions over the years. By the time Elite sent Baralinka to the "Rock" for covering sometime in 2011, his fees were reduced from the staggeringly high fee that had been charged when he first went to stud, but it still was a prestigious booking and would have cost a fair amount.

Rock of Gibraltar, in the early noughties, had been a world-champion racehorse. A dual Group One winning juvenile and then a five-time Group One winning three-year-old, he became the first horse to win seven consecutive group one races in the Northern hemisphere. This was a true blue blood, and although he would have been past his peak stud fee when Elite booked him, he still commanded a hefty fee. The *Racing Post* bloodstock records revealed that he was commanding a fee around €65,000 at his peak in 2004. By the time Elite booked him, the racehorse.com site suggested they paid just in excess of £14,000.

The reason the Rock had grabbed my attention initially had more to do with football than horse racing. Like Stan Hey, I was also a football supporter. Indeed, I was a season ticket holder at the Club that supplanted his favourites as the dominant team in British football, Manchester United. As a United supporter, I had well remembered the bitter dispute that existed around 2004 between the Club manager, Sir Alex Ferguson (the man almost solely responsible for United's preeminence) and the Irish racing tycoon, John Magnier. Without raking over the sad minutia of the dispute that had such serious repercussions for the club, it was essentially a disagreement about the stud fees accruing from the Rock of Gibraltar racehorse. Sir Alex had been part owner of the racehorse, but this dispute centred around the horse once it was retired to stud.

Whatever the rights and wrongs of the dispute, one thing was certain: it was front-page news at the time. The controversy, mixed with the bloodline, caused the Rock's stud fee to skyrocket. Despite the pedigree, it was often considered that at his peak, the Rock of Gibraltar was getting "silly money" for his stud fee.

Despite being past his peak when Elite obtained his services, I was fascinated by the prospect that Elite had in its string a horse whose bloodline went back to the horse at the centre of such controversy. Geology, as the horse was named, became the focus of my attention from 2013 onward as I waited to see how he might develop from yearling to racehorse.

In many ways, this last chapter became a very interesting one, not just in the vagaries of horse breeding but also in the fickle nature of this particular horse "ownership" model.

Beginning in January 2013, I started to take a real interest in the Baralinka–Rock of Gibraltar yearling, paying particular attention to all the breeding programme notes on how he was developing. Breeding is not an exact science. I well remember being told on a visit to the National Stud in Ireland what a hit-and-miss business it was, despite the money involved. Essentially, it appears to be about mixing the qualities inherent in the dam and the sire to produce a top-quality racehorse. To my uneducated eye, it seemed a question of mixing Baralinka's speed (she had been a useful sprinter, winning at six furlongs) with the Rock of Gibraltar's middle-distance ability (many of his Grade One wins were at a mile). In crude terms, if Geology developed these genetic traits, Elite would have some horse on its hands.

Initial reports were not encouraging. Reading between the lines, the yearling was proving to be a little disappointing in his physical development. He was considered small and behind the others in his group. Some of this was attributed to the fact that he was a "late" foaling. Although he was considered to be "short coupled" (short backed) and potentially strong, he was, in fact, quite weak—all in all, not a great specimen. He appeared to have a slight growth spurt in his second year, though, and I was pleased when he was consigned to the trainer Kevin Ryan, a top-class Northern flat trainer based at Malton, North Yorkshire. Ryan was in the leading ranks of flat trainers, having trained several Group One winners. I hoped he would be the man to oversee the development of Geology and bring out the potential of those all-important genes.

Improvement was evident, and suddenly there was talk that he might get a run in as a two-year-old toward the end of the 2014 season. Indeed, that was the case as Geology made his racecourse debut at Carlisle in August. It was a maiden stakes of five furlongs, and being a Class Five standard race, it was seen as hopefully a gentle introduction to the world of racing. With it being his first-ever run, quite a lot is taken on trust, and of course, if the breeding is right, then certain horses will be more favoured. Geology was the fourth favourite of ten horses. I snuck along to the bookies to see how this son of the Rock would make out, I decided to make my visit a watching brief. That proved to be a wise action because what followed was something of a disaster. Geology endured a baptism of fire; he seemed relatively clueless and slow, and he finished last. The *Racing Post*'s pithy description said, "Toward rear and outpaced, soon in rear and struggling." In an ordinary race, this was an uninspiring run. Rather alarmingly, Caties Do Dah finished ahead of him at 250–1. It was hard to take any positives out of such an underwhelming performance, but the trainer didn't seem too alarmed. There was much talk of "green" horses needing the experience, and so on. The consensus was that Geology would be put away for next season and allowed time to strengthen further.

I decided that, given the nature of the start to his racing career, it might be wise to seek the owner's badge sooner rather than later. Elite had become quite up front about their plans for horses in training and often listed their long-term plans in terms of whether the horses would be kept or not. Despite the trainer's comments, there were clearly some reservations about Geology's prospects, and even at this early stage, it was clear he might not last long. I decided that wherever he was running at the start of the 2015 flat season, I would endeavor to obtain an owner's badge. All the trainer's reports at the start of the year were promising enough, and the horse was stronger and doing better on the gallops. Kevin Ryan mentioned a few possible entries in April, and then news came through that Geology was declared to run at Pontefract on Monday, April 20. It was a six-furlong maiden stakes, and I was determined to go and see the son of Rock of Gibraltar.

So, without further hesitation, I applied in the usual manner and confidently awaited the response. I had enjoyed fantastic luck in my owner's strategy so far, getting to Haydock, Longchamp, Bangor, and Carlisle almost according to plan. However, this was the point when Mr. Hey might have said, "Told you so," as my application was rejected. The thousands of members' argument had gone against me this time. However, I wasn't going to be deterred, I would go and see Geology anyway and put in for an owner's badge later in the season. The fact that I am now about to give a detailed résumé of Geology's run at Pontefract, in the same template as the four previous race days, might give some indication of what a sad and frustrating season was to be had with the unfortunate Geology.

• • •

RACE DAY—GEOLOGY AT PONTEFRACT, MONDAY, APRIL 20, 2015
THE RACECOURSE

In his informative guide to British racecourses written in 2001, Alan Lee described the Pontefract racecourse as a "working man's" track. Most of the "work" done in this town's industrial heyday is long since gone, with the coal mining that was the backbone of employment decimated by closures in the 1990s. The last colliery closed in 2002. A quirky tradition at the course had been that afternoon racing used to be put back to a start time of 2:45 p.m. to accommodate miners coming off the early shift. This was clearly not necessary anymore, and the card for a Monday meeting in late April was due to start at 2:10 p.m. However, there was clearly a healthy appetite for the races here. A good crowd had assembled for this start of the "working week" meeting.

Once you got away from the busy roads and concrete blocks that characterise modern Pontefract, you are in for a pleasant surprise because the course is located in a rural oasis of pleasant parkland. This is an impressive course, with a long, tree-lined approach to some splendidly ornate turnstiles. The course is similarly impressive beyond the turnstiles, with a tidy parade ring recessed to the left and a winner's enclosure (where I didn't expect to see Geology) on the other side of the path. This is a hilly course, Alan Lee had described the jockeys climbing "up a path from the weighing room to the paddock, where horses plod ready for the one in three incline on every circuit." I was "roughing it" on this day. Without my owner's badge, I would not be able to access Pontefract's owner's facilities, but I was happy enough with the impressive grandstand and paddock that I had paid my way into. This enabled a good vantage point to take in quite a panoramic view of the two-mile oval course that appeared below me. This stand had a pleasant enough dining room located on the top of the grandstand, and on this cool April day, I enjoyed an ample portion of the staple—pie and chips.

Looking down the course, I wondered how Geology was going to deal with this track. Timeform had emphasised the considerable gradient involved and the stiff uphill finish. Stamina rather than speed might be critical, especially over that tough three-furlong finish.

• • •

PRERACE
I had no fellow "owners" to locate on this day, but I had noted that the preparade ring adjoining the parade ring was a large, spacious area. In advance of Geology's race, I positioned myself there. While I was waiting for Geology to appear, I took stock of the less-than-flattering assessment of the horse in both the race programme and the *Racing Post*. The programme noted the Rock of Gibraltar sire and that Geology was related to some "winners." The writer had said he "looked clueless on sole juvenile start but must be capable of better." The *Racing Post* offered even less encouragement, saying, "Very green last of ten at Carlisle maiden in August, bred to do much better at some stage, but will need to see good money for him before getting involved." The breeding, of course, was the reason for

my interest, but "good money" certainly wasn't appearing, as poor Geology drifted out to 50–1.

Kevin Ryan's comments the week before the race had offered some encouragement, though; he had talked in terms of "starting points" and "bringing him on."

None of the adverse comment seemed to have affected Geology; he plodded around the preparade seemingly without a care in the world. I wondered if the almost mandatory gelding operation he had undergone in the past had worked a little too well. Although not exactly on his toes, he looked healthy enough as he passed into the main parade ring. This time, I wasn't privy to any last-minute instructions between trainer and jockey, but I did note that Mr. Ryan obviously had more pressing engagements, because he wasn't there.

It was obvious to me, though, that on this day, I was supporting a hopeless case. Loyalty dictated a bet, and I modified my each-way bet accordingly.

This appeared a modest maiden, but most of the horses appeared to be more favoured than our son of the Rock. Richard Fahey's Beardwood was a hot favourite.

• • •

THE RACE—MAIDEN STAKES (CLASS FIVE, 3+ YEARS OLD) 6 FURLONGS

Geology was drawn tenth of the eleven runners, not altogether encouraging given that lower-drawn horses were favoured. I trained the binoculars on him at the start, and he appeared to break well enough and seemed to be up with the pack, in middivision for the first couple of furlongs. This was a six-furlong sprint, so bearing in mind my earlier thoughts on stamina, I felt that if he could stay with them, we might see a surprise at the finish. Such thoughts were instantly redundant, as Geology seemed to be almost moving on the spot as all the others got away from him, leaving him stone last. He cut a disconsolate figure, clearly unable to improve his situation as he was badly outpaced by the field. He managed a minor rally in the final few strides and passed a couple of horses to finish ninth.

Beardwood proved to be a worthy favourite and won the race well. Tom Dascombe's Dawn's Early Light came second and Roger Varian's Marsasim was third.

• • •

POSTRACE
There was no escaping it; this was a poor performance by Geology in a Class Five maiden, and for a horse on the "sell" list, it did not bode well for his future prospects.

I wandered back to the parade ring, which was deserted. Sometime later, to my surprise, Geology appeared in the ring and was scrubbed down and watered by his handlers. He was inauspiciously positioned in front of the veterinary offices, but he seemed fine. Not being with the owner's group, I had no idea where they had their debrief, but given the horse's appearance, it must have been a short one. With all the winning connections and fuss on the other side of the path, Geology cooled down in glorious isolation. He had sweated up, but not excessively. As the handler left the parade ring, I asked her how he had done. She seemed relatively pleased. The inference seemed to be that he was inexperienced, that he was learning the game. I concluded that he would have to learn it a good deal quicker if he was going to be around for long. Kevin Ryan's comments a few days later were similarly positive; overall, he seemed pleased with the horse's efforts. He made reference to his pleasing finish and presumably saw something to build on.

I decided that if the trainer still retained confidence, I should go up to Hambleton Lodge on a club visit and see the horse on the gallops (a training run).

• • •

POSTSCRIPT—GEOLOGY

Before I could go see Geology at his training base, he was declared to race again in May at Thirsk. This was a seven-furlong maiden, and Geology gave a more encouraging account of himself. He led the eight-horse field with some vigour and although outpaced at the end, he ended up winning a tiny bit of prize money, finishing fourth at 33–1. So it was with a sense of increased optimism that I visited Kevin Ryan's Hambleton Lodge stables early one freezing June morning. Mr. Ryan runs a big operation, and a sizeable group of horses made their way up his impressive gallops. His stables must be among the highest in the country in terms of altitude. It took quite a hike to reach the highest point. If nothing else, it must make his horses among the toughest in the country.

Later, the trainer and his assistants paraded Geology along with all his star horses at the stables. There was some guarded optimism regarding Geology's future prospects. The BHA had announced his handicap mark, and the modest seventy one figure was considered "fair."

Frustratingly, I was on holiday when Geology appeared a few days later at Doncaster, competing in a Class Four handicap over a mile. Again, Geology went to the front early but faded over the greater distance, finishing sixth of the ten runners. In late July, I was a little surprised to see Geology declared to run at Windsor, this time in a Class Five handicap over a mile. Already the handicapper had dropped his mark to 68. It was a small field of five, and I assumed that Geology wouldn't have been sent so far if the trainer didn't think this was a good opportunity for the horse. Again I was away, but it was an evening meeting, and I slipped into the bookies to see if he could finally make a breakthrough in his racing career. Three of the others were ahead of Geology in the betting, but as the *Sporting Life* pointed out, "Geology won't be traveling from Yorkshire without good reason." Geology certainly started with some intent, leading the field in his usual manner, but all too quickly the others caught him. He faded, finishing a well-beaten fourth. This was another deflating experience, for horse and connections.

I had considered that I would "get in" to see Geology before his season ended. It was only July, and Kevin Ryan often ran horses like this right up until October. However, given the disappointing nature of this performance, I began to wonder if such an opportunity might not exist. To make matters worse, Geology sustained some injuries, and a poisoned foot meant there were to be no races in August. However, a slightly better performance in Geology's next race in September made me feel that I would get to see him before his season was done. I was booked elsewhere again, but Geology finished sixth in a fourteen-runner handicap at Ayr.

There had been talk that he might have a run on the all-weather race tracks, and I checked out the route to Lingfield or Wolverhampton. However, all these hopes were dashed some days later, when there was a short announcement in the newsletter that Geology was being entered in the "horses in training" sale at Doncaster in October. So rather than going to see Geology one last time, I instead had the prospect of seeing what I suppose could be the end of Geology's short racing career at the Doncaster sale.

I considered that it would be too much of an anticlimax to appear in person, so I settled down to watch the semisurreal experience of the sale online. It's an auction like any other, with the horses for sale paraded in a small ring like an amphitheatre, with a smattering of people watching and the auctioneer with his gavel at the ready. Elite had got into the habit of selling horses now. For years, it had seemed that they just raced them, and then they were packed off to "good homes." However, commercial imperatives now seemed to dictate a more robust policy. Only a few weeks before, a similarly unimpressive flat horse of theirs had fetched £16,000, which was considered very reasonable.

Geology was listed as being in Lot 158 and was due to be sold the day before bonfire night.

While I waited for the horse to appear, I read through his listing in the catalogue. His breeding details were presented in bold type, with reference not just to Rock of Gibraltar and Baralinka, but to Kalinka as well. The performance list looked sparse: "Six starts, one place, £385." The last three runs were there, along with that modest BHA mark of 65. These performance figures were hardly likely to raise many bids, but given my initial interest in the sire, I waited to see the outcome. This is not the major sale that takes place at Newmarket, so I watched the earlier proceedings to see what kind of prices were being fixed. Despite the auctioneer trying to get the bids up into the five-figure area, many horses seemed to settle around a couple of thousand, although some fetched appreciably more.

By late afternoon, Geology appeared, looking in many ways very similar to his appearance at Pontefract: relaxed and well turned out. The auctioneer, as in his previous manner, tried to get the bidding off at a high level, but quickly reverted to the base level of two thousand pounds. He name-checked Rock of Gibraltar and quickly affirmed that Geology was related to the great Soviet Song. Almost as an afterthought, he reminded the audience that the horse had been placed this year. I watched sadly as absolutely no bids appeared to be made. After an interminable wait, he announced a bid: £800. He tried to use this as a starting point, but no further bids appeared imminent. So he plaintively added, "My one and only bid. Any more?" The gavel came down, Geology had been sold for £800.

It had been a long time since Rock of Gibraltar's stud fee had peaked, and I well remembered what the man at the Irish National Stud had told me about the finicky nature of horse breeding. In terms of his progeny, of course the Rock could number hundreds of horses, and Coolmore proudly listed his more famous Group One winners, including Samitar and Society Rock. Given all the bitter recriminations and charges of over ten years before regarding Rock of Gibraltar's stud fees, the irony of Geology's rock-bottom price did not escape me.

7
Postscript

ONE OF THE things that always amused me when mentioning my involvement with horses for this exercise over the past couple of years was people's conception of horse ownership. People assume that horse ownership is the preserve of the landed gentry or the *nouveau riche*. Although this remains true to some extent, it doesn't tell the whole story. I'm slightly taking the mickey when I tell them I "own" a horse, but their reaction remains the same: "I thought you had to be dead rich to do that." Of course the majority of people know that my financial status could never be described as that. However, what the "shoestring" approach shows is that no matter how small, it is possible to have an interest in a horse that enables you to enjoy all the aspects of full-time ownership. I suppose this tells us that the self-democratisation of horse ownership that Stan Hey mentioned in the nineties has become established and, to some extent, has been a success.

Outside of the very top echelons of owners, I don't think owners make much, if any, money from racing. In that sense it is a rich man or woman's hobby. Certainly, my little cross section of horses reflected the quixotic nature of the racing game. They had their ups and downs, and overall they did return a small amount of money in relation to their initial costs. Stan Hey had itemised all of his spending over his "ownership" period very explicitly. He had a much bigger share in a number of horses; therefore, his outgoings were appreciably more than mine, as were his entertainment expenses along the way. If I remember correctly, his expenses exceeded £7,000. I don't remember any of his horses winning prize money, although, of course, that was the nub of the story.

Over the two years, my "shoestring" expenses were just over £500, and my prize-money return was just over £73 (a return of about 15 percent). Although I have no way of knowing what sort of returns more serious "owners" obtain, I have the distinct impression that, for the majority, it would not be as good.

So why, then, do people do it, if in the majority of cases they will only get a meagre return on their input? Well, some of them are very rich people, and they can clearly afford to subsidise their hobby and passion. However, even though I was an owner on the most micro scale possible, I gleaned the reasons that underlie the accounts sheet. It wasn't really about money; it was about the sheer joy of the occasion. It was the different level of involvement with "your" horse, whether it was news from the training yard or the performance on the track. It was about going to such a range of different racecourses, all boasting their different characteristics and history. It was about seeing first-hand how a trainer or a jockey operates in this most unforgiving of sports. It was about shouting yourself hoarse (no pun intended) as your steed galloped up towards the finish, whether that was at Longchamp or Cartmel. It was about meeting all those people who make a day at the races so unique, whether it's a word with Lord Cavendish or some of your fellow "owners." It was about relishing that glass of champagne or that slice of home-made pie.

In sum, it's about being part of the "game"—you are involved in the magical world of horse racing.

Overall, I would judge my exercise in horse "ownership" a success, and it has encouraged me to continue with it and to become even more involved in terms of share ownership. How else could I ever have turned up in the ring at Longchamp on Arc day or supported "my" horse at Haydock on Lancashire chase day? Tongue would be planted firmly in cheek when I'd annoy my friends by saying, "As Lord Cavendish said to me...." Meeting such a wide range of racing folk would certainly not have been possible if this exercise had not taken place. Being able to empathise with Ruth Jefferson's frustration as Chilly came up short at Bangor gives one an insight into the real nature of the game that is not visible to the outside punter. I didn't really encounter Stan Heys's difficulty with officialdom at racecourses; most were welcoming and professional in their dealings. None were more so than Carlisle. When Bruno ran, we really couldn't have asked for a more hospitable welcome. Even Geology's difficult season had its interest, as once again it offered a relatively unique insight into the difficulties most trainers face in just getting their horses to the racecourse.

The Own a Racehorse (OAR) organisation turned out to be what they said on their straightforward website. Their communications were excellent, and even if it is most unlikely that they will get their horses to the spring festivals, they do get their horses and their "owners" to the races, and they do win races. Bruno was a fascinating insight into racing at, shall we say, a more mundane level. He was an honest trier who had developed quite a loyal following. These people were there in strength at Carlisle, and although he was not at his best that day, they all seemed to enjoy the day at the races that he provided. As Mr. Hey found out, some horses may run on multiple occasions without ever winning, but Bruno, after waiting for nearly three years, managed the feat, and that was some achievement. The Racegoers Club proved to be a very worthwhile organisation, in addition to my experiences with their ownership syndicates. Theirs is a serious and worthwhile attempt to raise and sustain the profile of horse racing by getting people to attend races. Looking at the crowds I encountered on my journeys, I think they are succeeding.

In terms of syndicates I found them to be a democratic, well-run organisation that offer a good product at a very reasonable price. Above all, they succeeded in always being able to get their "owners" to the races, providing multiple opportunities to go to various race-courses. Chilly Miss was a grand syndicate horse in that she raced on numerous occasions and always gave the "owners" a run for their money, winning and retaining the ability to improve yet further. Elite Racing Club's longevity probably reflects their success at bringing a micro version of "ownership" to the masses. Over the years, the success of their horses speaks for itself.

The real success of this operation is the fact that they breed their own horses. In this modern world of the Coolmore and Emirati racehorse owners, this is no minor achievement. The three horses I chose from their string all were their homebreds. And although they enjoyed vastly different fortunes over the time period, the fact that one of them, Ribbons, became their first Group One winner since Soviet Song was very special. The club lost one of its key foundation mares (Kalinka) in 2014 and its most famous horse (Soviet Song) in 2015, so to see Ribbons, who was linked to that bloodline, do so well was very gratifying.

Doyly Carte might have "fallen out of love" with racing, but she was a good class hurdler in her prime that provided wonderful memories from Haydock. Even Geology's ill-fated career was an interesting story in terms of the genetic bloodlines that had interested me.

So to finish where I started, I would concur fully with Stan Hey's conclusion that "putting a value" on these wider characteristics of horse "ownership" is indeed unquantifiable and is the very essence of what the racing game is all about.

It's clear to me that prize money, particularly at the grassroots level, is hopelessly inadequate. Prize money clearly does not equate to training costs for the majority of owners. Small investors will clearly have to limit themselves to smaller meetings, while a few bigger ones will dine at the top table. To some extent, though, the days of one or two very rich large investors is done, it would seem to me that they alone cannot sustain horse racing in the modern day. The way forward could well be for the BHA to do even more to promote horse-owners' groups, in the manner of the RGC. The "ownership on a shoestring" model is a modest vehicle, but it can clearly help "owners" make horse racing worthwhile. This is good news for the smaller investor wanting to dabble in horse ownership. It may still be the sport of kings, but it is possible to be king for a day.

Glossary

FOR THE UNINITIATED below are a list of terms used in the book, which you may find helpful.

BHA – British Horseracing Authority

Black Type – a horse that has won or been placed in a pattern/listed race, usually enhances their breeding value.

Bumper – national hunt flat race for prospective jumping horses

Connections – owners and trainers of a horse.

Cut in the ground – the ground surface that has been softened by rain.

Dam – the mother of a horse.

Declared – a horse is confirmed to start in a race (usually 48 hours in advance for flat horses and 24 hours for jumps).

Frame – horses finishing in the first three places.

Furlong – one eighth of a mile or 220 yards and the distance in which races are measured.

Gelding – a male horse that has been castrated.

Going – official description of the racing surface, it is determined by the amount of moisture in the ground. This can range from heavy, soft, good and firm.

Graded races – the top tier of races. On the flat group 1 is the highest category, with group 2 and 3 in descending order. Over the jumps, the top tier is grade 1 with grade 2 and 3 in descending order.

Green – an inexperienced horse

Handicap – the BHA allocate a different weight for each horse to carry. After a horse has run usually three times it is allocated an official handicap mark that determines the weight it will carry in a handicap race.

Juvenile – two year old horse

Listed race – a class of race just below group (flat) or graded (jumps).

Maiden – a horse that hasn't yet won a race.

Napped – best bet according to a tipster

Odds on – strong favourite, where winnings are less than the stake

Placepot – selecting a placed horse in all 6 races at a selected race meeting.

Pulled up – a horse that drops out of the race, a non-finisher.

Rating – a measure of a horse's ability usually on a scale from 0 to over 100. There are different official rating figures for flat and national hunt horses.

Ring – parade ring where connections meet as horse parades.

Sire – father of a horse.

String – all the horses in a particular training stable.

Timber – racing over hurdles

Yearling – a horse of either sex during 1 January to 31 December following the year of its birth.

 Having spent an enjoyable career teaching sixth form students for over thirty years, Steve was lucky enough to obtain early retirement in 2011. Despite the demands of the job and helping to bring up three children, Steve managed to find the time to write two books on his first sporting passion football. He has put his increased leisure time to good effect by intensifying his interest in horse racing. It was while travelling around British, Irish and French racecourses that he came up with the idea of writing his third book;" Four Hooves and a Prayer". Steve lives in Manchester with his wife Sue.

46448836R00054

Printed in Poland
by Amazon Fulfillment
Poland Sp. z o.o., Wrocław